Integrative and Interdisciplinary Curriculum in the Middle School

Originally published as a special issue of the *Middle School Journal*, this book presents integrative curriculum as a foundational element of the middle school.

By addressing the current gap in literature on curriculum integration in the middle grades, this text explores how learning can be organized around authentic concepts or questions which cut across disciplines and speak to young adolescents. Providing a current, nuanced, and comprehensive review of what it means to embrace and implement an interdisciplinary and integrative curriculum, the volume considers how educators can create and deliver a high-quality integrative curriculum which is enjoyable, challenging, and inclusive. Examples of implementation in teacher preparation programs and middle grade classrooms showcase integrative approaches and illustrate how curricula have been key in tackling social inequities, increasing engagement with STEM, and supporting collaboration.

This text will be of great interest to graduate and postgraduate students, researchers, academics, and libraries in the field of Middle School Education, Curriculum Studies, Teacher Education, Theories of Learning, and STEM Education.

Lisa M. Harrison is Associate Professor of Teacher Education at the Patton College of Education at Ohio University, US.

Ellis Hurd is Professor of Teaching and Learning at the College of Education, Illinois State University, US.

Kathleen Brinegar is Associate Professor of Education at Northern Vermont University, US.

Routledge Research in Education

This series aims to present the latest research from right across the field of education. It is not confined to any particular area or school of thought and seeks to provide coverage of a broad range of topics, theories and issues from around the world.

Recent titles in the series include:

Legacies of Christian Languaging and Literacies in American Education
Perspectives on English Language Arts Curriculum, Teaching and Learning
Edited by Mary M. Juzwik, Jennifer C. Stone, Kevin J. Burke, and Denise Dávila

Critical Explorations of Young Adult Literature
Identifying and Critiquing the Canon
Edited by Victor Malo-Juvera and Crag Hill

Dance, Professional Practice, and the Workplace
Challenges and Opportunities for Dance Professionals, Students, and Educators
Edited by Angela Pickard and Doug Risner

Pedagogy in the Novels of J.M. Coetzee
The Affect of Literature
Aparna Mishra Tarc

Integrative and Interdisciplinary Curriculum in the Middle School
Integrated Approaches in Teacher Preparation and Practice
Edited by Lisa M. Harrison, Ellis Hurd, and Kathleen Brinegar

Integrative and Interdisciplinary Curriculum in the Middle School

Integrated Approaches in Teacher Preparation and Practice

Edited by Lisa M. Harrison, Ellis Hurd, and Kathleen Brinegar

Routledge
Taylor & Francis Group

NEW YORK AND LONDON

First published 2020
by Routledge
605 Third Avenue, New York, NY 10017

and by Routledge
2 Park Square, Milton Park, Abingdon, Oxon, OX14 4RN

First issued in paperback 2021

Routledge is an imprint of the Taylor & Francis Group, an informa business

Library of Congress Cataloging-in-Publication Data
A catalog record for this book has been requested

ISBN 13: 978-1-03-223833-3 (pbk)
ISBN 13: 978-0-367-37044-2 (hbk)

Typeset in Sabon
by Apex CoVantage, LLC

Contents

Contributors

Amy Atkinson, M.S., is the middle school librarian at Latin School of Chicago. E-mail: amy.lynn.atkinson@gmail.com

William P. Bintz, Ph.D., is a professor in the Department of Teaching, Leadership, and Curriculum Studies at Kent State University, Kent, OH. E-mail: wbintz@kent.edu

Heather Coffey, Ph.D., is an associate professor in the Department of Middle, Secondary, and K12 Education at Cato College of Education. She serves as director of the University of North Carolina (UNC) Charlotte Writing Project, Charlotte, NC. E-mail: hcoffey@uncc.edu

Danielle Dani, Ed.D., is associate professor in the Department of Teacher Education at Ohio University. E-mail: dani@ohio.edu

Sharlene Denos, Ph.D., is Associate Director of Education and Inclusivity at the Center for the Physics of Living Cells at University of Illinois at Urbana-Champaign. E-mail: denos@illinois.edu

Lia D. Falco, Ph.D., is an assistant professor in the Disability & Psycho-educational Studies Department at the University of Arizona. Email: ldf@email.arizona.edu

Steve Fulton is an English language arts teacher at Kannapolis Middle School, Kannapolis, NC. E-mail: steve.fulton@kcs.k12.nc.us

Shelly Furuness, Ph.D., is an Associate Professor and Curriculum Coordinator in the College of Education at Butler University. Email: sfurunes@butler.edu

Peggy F. Hopper, Ph.D., is professor in the Department of Curriculum, Instruction, and Special Education at Mississippi State University. E-mail: pfh7@colled.msstate.edu

Jessica Ivy, Ph.D., is assistant professor of STEM Education in the Annsley Frazier Thornton School of Education at Bellarmine University. E-mail: jivy@bellarmine.edu

Gumiko Monobe, Ph.D., is an assistant professor in the Department of Teaching, Leadership, and Curriculum Studies at Kent State University, Kent, OH. E-mail: gmonobe@kent.edu.

Kelly M. Moser, Ph.D., is assistant professor in the Department of Classical & Modern Languages and Literatures at Mississippi State University. E-mail: kellymoser@cmll.msstate.edu

Kathy Rodems, M.S., is an English instructor at the University Laboratory High School at University of Illinois at Urbana-Champaign. E-mail: krodems@illinois.edu

Michelle Rupenthal, M.S., is a doctoral student at Indiana University and an adjunct instructor at Butler University. Email: mrupenth@butler.edu

Ryan Summers, Ph.D., is Assistant Professor of science education in the Department of Teaching, Leadership, and Professional Practice at University of North Dakota. E-mail: ryan.summers@und.edu

Introduction

Lisa M. Harrison, Ellis Hurd, and Kathleen Brinegar

Propelling the middle school movement was the implementation of a conceptual framework made up of organizational structures and principles designed to support the developmental characteristics and needs of young adolescents. One of the foundational components of this conceptual framework is curriculum integration through interdisciplinary teams (Ellerbrock, Falbe, & Franz, 2018). During the middle school movement, curriculum integration became a distinguishing factor in separating the newly developed middle school model from the junior high school model that mostly replicated the practices seen within high schools. While the junior high school model was defined by subject-centered curriculum, an emphasis on cognitive development, and the departmentalization of content, the middle school model centered on student-oriented curriculum that focused on both cognitive and affective development, and was interdisciplinary in nature (Powell, 2014).

Specifically, the middle school movement gave way to reimagining curriculum for young adolescents, which was "distinguished by learning experiences that address societal expectations while appealing to young adolescents and offering them opportunities to pose and answer questions that are important to them" (National Middle School Association [NMSA], 2010, p. 17). This vision of curriculum is integrative and is implemented by interdisciplinary teams of educators.

Integrative teaching is beneficial to middle-level learners because it provides young adolescents the opportunity to explore and synthesize understandings about themselves and society through multiple lenses. While there has been an abundance of literature published on integrative curriculum throughout the middle school movement, Nagle et al. (2018) stated that since 2000, the current research that explores integrative curriculum in relation to student learning has become scarce. One notable exception to the absence of research was the issue on integrative curriculum and practices published in volume 50, issue 2 of the *Middle School Journal*. This monograph, *Integrative and interdisciplinary curriculum in the middle school: Integrated approaches in teacher preparation and practice* builds on *Middle School Journal's* issue to address the current gap in the literature on curriculum integration in the middle grades. The special issue was expanded into this edited book by compiling the four chapters from the issue and three additional articles found in the *Middle School Journal* to provide a current, nuanced, and comprehensive review of an interdisciplinary and integrative curriculum.

What Is an Interdisciplinary and Integrated Curriculum?

Within middle level education, Beane's (1990) conceptualization of curriculum integration has set a precedent on how middle-level educators think about and implement curriculum. According to Beane (1997):

> Curriculum integration is a curriculum design that is concerned with enhancing the possibilities for personal and social integration through the organization of curriculum around significant problems and issues, collaboratively identified by educators and young people, without regard for subject-area boundaries.
>
> (pp. x–xi)

Powell (2014) noted that there is variance between the terms interdisciplinary and integrated/integrative curriculum. In this regard, (a) where interdisciplinary focuses on teacher-centered planning, integrated focuses on teacher- and student-driven learning; (b) integrated weaves together the core subjects into seamless lessons whereas interdisciplinary only attempts to blur the boundaries between the subjects; and (c) where interdisciplinary is conceptual in its focus, integrated is thematic and explores much more flexible content "connected to student's lives" (Powell, 2014, p. 162). In fact, it is only in integrated curriculum that we see the essential problems of society or an inquiry-based education thrive because it is the students themselves who are driving the learning and extension of content based on their own interests.

As educators, we should strive to make school an enjoyable and inclusive space for all students. Designing units and lessons that are engaging is important; however, that should not be the sole standard in which educators measure quality curriculum. In addition to being engaging, middle-level practitioners should strive to create a curriculum that is "challenging, exploratory, integrative, and relevant" (NMSA, 2010, p. 17). More so, middle-level educators should seek to design curriculum that is connected to youth's lived experiences, a core principle of integrated curriculum. When we root curriculum in supporting students to make meaning of everyday life, the curriculum inherently becomes integrated, as the human experience is dynamic, multifaceted, and interdisciplinary. Building curriculum on everyday experiences also provides a meaningful entry point to learning for young adolescents.

Beane's (1997) vision of integrated curriculum is bold in that he pushes educators to not only view curriculum as a tool for learning but also a tool for change. He argued that integrated curriculum should focus both on inquiry and action. An integrated curriculum should help foster and develop youth's critical thinking skills while also preparing them to be active citizens in a democracy. Collectively, if students are engaged in an authentic integrative curriculum approach, then they should come away with a heightened understanding of their personal lived experiences, an increased understanding of the historical, social, and cultural context that shapes society, and skill sets that they can use to enact change.

Organization of This Book

The research within this book speaks to the benefits of engaging in curriculum integration and also offers practical guidelines for educators who might be interested in implementing integrative curriculum. The first four chapters present scholarship centered in middle grades classrooms, while the last three chapters focus on middle-level teacher preparation. Though each chapter has a specific focus, conceptually, each chapter offers research that is beneficial to teacher educators and middle school teachers alike.

In Chapter 1, Coffey and Fulton explore how engaging middle school students in a critical service learning project helped students to develop a social justice mindset, improve their writing skills, and encouraged them to think more deeply about the injustices within their own community context. Rupenthal and Furuness follow in Chapter 2 and share a case study of one school's year-long process of implementing curriculum integration. Specifically, their chapter highlights how one eighth-grade teacher enacted integrated curriculum across five English classes through the support of a Professional Learning Community. In Chapter 3, Falco applies aspects of curriculum integration to support young adolescent girls' self-efficacy in mathematics. She took up this integrative approach to counteract the gender inequities seen within the mathematics field by empowering girls with the skills and dispositions needed to be successful in math and in other areas of their lives. Chapter 4 includes how Summers, Rodems, Denos, and Atkinson also used an integrative approach to support STEM learning. They share how a librarian, science, and English teacher collaborated to implement an integrated scientific argumentation unit framed around the essential question: Where might we find life outside of Earth in our solar system? This chapter highlights the collective strength that results from a collaborative interdisciplinary process.

Beginning with Chapter 5, we transition to middle-level teacher preparation. Bintz and Monobe share research from a graduate education course consisting of practicing teachers across different disciplines. Within the course, graduate students used poetry to integrate reading and writing across the curriculum. In Chapter 6, Moser, Ivy, and Hopper highlight the value of interdisciplinary collaboration among teacher education faculty to support preservice teachers' development of meaningful themes explorable across disciplines. Finally, in Chapter 7, Dani demonstrates how place-based education can serve as a valuable pedagogical approach to support curriculum integration. In addition, her work provides examples of how place-based education assists preservice teachers to develop an asset-based perspective of middle grades students' local context.

What's Next

Beane (1995) argued, "the central focus of curriculum integration is the search for self and social meaning" (p. 616). To fully engage in curriculum integration, it is important for educators to have a deep understanding of young adolescents and their position within the larger world. This first comes with addressing our own biases and developing our cultural competencies as educators. The reality is that the majority of teachers will not teach students who are exactly like them and will experience the world in a vastly different way than their students. These distinct experiences might be due to differences in ethnicity, gender, socioeconomic status, ability, sexuality, religion, or family structure. As we engage in integrative practices, we also need to make sure that our practices are developmentally responsive, culturally responsive, and equitable.

Similar to the calls to meet the developmental needs of young adolescents that started the middle school movement and resulted in creating school structures such as interdisciplinary teaming, there is a new call within middle-level education that urges educators to meet the cultural needs of young adolescents (Brinegar, Harrison, & Hurd, 2019; Kennedy, Brinegar, Hurd, & Harrison, 2016). This long overdue call is rooted in creating equitable student outcomes and being responsive to the changing education landscape, which recognizes more ethnic and linguistic student diversity than what existed during the start of the middle school movement. If the heart of the middle school movement is really centered on creating schools specifically designed for all young adolescents, middle-level educators must examine whether the grounding practices support the diversity of student identity and experience present in schools today. The research presented within this book demonstrates that integrative practices are still relevant and valuable in supporting students' academic development. More so, the research in this book also points to the utility of curriculum integration in answering middle-level education's new call for equitable teaching practices to support young adolescents.

While the chapters in this book gives us hope, it is important to recognize the need for continuous research on integrated curriculum. There has been an increased phasing out of middle-level practices such as curriculum integration by schools due to the pressures of high-stakes testing rolled out during the No Child Left Behind era and that still persist after the passing of the Every Student Succeeds Act (Faulkner & Cook, 2006; Huss & Eastep, 2011). Additional research on how curriculum integration actually functions to support achievement is necessary if middle-level advocates hope to elevate the importance and value of the middle school concept.

In light of middle-level education's current focus on equity, new research is also needed that shows how integrative curriculum aligns with and can help achieve equitable educational outcomes for all young adolescents. In a review of the literature on middle-level practices, Hurd, Harrison, Brinegar, and Kennedy (2018) found that much of the research on curriculum integration took a color-blind approach and did not work towards disrupting oppressive educational practices. As demonstrated in chapters within this book and other middle-level research (see Brown & Leaman, 2007; Milne, 2016) curriculum integration is a powerful tool in supporting culturally responsive curricular practices, however more research is needed to show how educators can use curriculum integration to help students think about their own positionality and critically reflect on the world around them.

Conclusion

The intent of this book is to disseminate current research on curriculum integration in the middle grades. The chapters within this book reflect how curriculum integration has been implemented in middle grades classrooms and in middle-level teacher preparation. It demonstrates that thoughtfully implemented integrative curriculum can serve as a powerful approach to engage students in social problem-solving, to challenge students to see the relevance and interconnectedness of what they are learning, and to support their cultivation of a sense of social agency. As you read and reflect on this scholarship, we challenge you to not only incorporate curriculum integration within your own practice, but to also reflect upon other compatible pedagogical approaches that will leave students more knowledgeable, passionate about learning, civically engaged, and justice oriented.

References

Beane, J. A. (1990). *A middle school curriculum: From rhetoric to reality*. Columbus, OH: National Middle School Association.

Beane, J. A. (1995). Curriculum integration and the disciplines of knowledge. *Phi Delta Kappan*, 76(8), 616–622.

Beane, J. A. (1997). *Curriculum integration: Designing the core of democratic education*. New York: Teachers College Press.

Brinegar, K. M., Harrison, L. M., & Hurd, E. (2019). *Equity and cultural responsiveness in the middle grades*. Charlotte, NC: Information Age Publications.

Brown, D. F., & Leaman, H. L. (2007). Recognizing and responding to young adolescents' ethnic identity development. In S. B. Mertens, V. A. Anfara, & M. M. Caskey (Eds.), *The young adolescent and the middle school*. Charlotte, NC: Information Age Publishing.

Ellerbrock, C., Falbe, K. N., & Franz, D. P. (2018). Middle grades schools and structures. In S. B. Mertens & M. M. Caskey (Eds.), *Literature reviews in support of the middle level education research agenda* (pp. 203–230). Charlotte, NC: Information Age Publishing.

Faulkner, S. A., & Cook, C. M. (2006). Testing vs. teaching: The perceived impact of assessment demands on middle grades instructional practices. *RMLE Online, 29*(7), 1–13.

Hurd, E., Harrison, L., Brinegar, K., & Kennedy, B. L. (2018). Cultural responsiveness in the middle grades: a literature review. In S. B. Mertens & M. M. Caskey (Eds.), *Literature reviews in support of the middle level education research agenda* (pp. 25–51). Charlotte, NC: Information Age Publishing.

Huss, J. A., & Eastep, S. (2011). A tri-state study: Is the middle school movement thriving . . . or barely surviving? *RMLE Online, 34*(9), 1–13.

Kennedy, B. L., Brinegar, K., Hurd, E., & Harrison, L. (2016). Synthesizing middle grades research on cultural responsiveness: The importance of a shared conceptual framework. *Middle Grades Review, 2*(3), 1–20. Retrieved from http://scholarworks.uvm.edu/mgreview/vol2/iss3/2

Milne, A. (2016). Where am I in our schools' White spaces? Social justice for the learners we marginalize. *Middle Grades Review, 1*(3), 1–9.

Nagle, J. F., Lemley, S. M., Swanson, K. W., Schaefer, M., Falbe, K. N., Netcoh, St., & Smith, K. W. (2018). The state of curriculum in the middle grades. In S. B. Mertens & M. M. Caskey (Eds.), *Literature reviews in support of the middle level education research agenda* (pp. 25–51). Charlotte, NC: Information Age Publishing.

National Middle School Association. (2010). *This we believe: Keys to educating young adolescents*. Westerville, OH: Author.

Powell, S. D. (2014). *Introduction to middle school* (3rd ed.). Upper Saddle River, NJ: Pearson.

Section I
Scholarship Centered in Middle Grades Classrooms

1 The Responsible Change Project

Building a Justice-Oriented Middle School Curriculum Through Critical Service-Learning

Heather Coffey and Steve Fulton

This We Believe Characteristics

- Educators value young adolescents and are prepared to teach them.
- Curriculum is challenging, exploratory, integrative, and relevant.
- A shared vision developed by all stakeholders guides every decision.
- The school includes community and business partners.

In the summer of 2016, a National Writing Project (NWP) site in the southeastern United States received funding from a US Department of Education Supporting Effective Educator Development (SEED) grant to conduct professional development with practicing teachers around argument writing through the College Ready Writers Program (now College, Career, and Community Writers Program, or C3WP). During this intensive 10-day summer institute, 12 teachers participated in activities and discussions that focused on source-based argument writing using a variety of texts for support. Through the use of routine argument writing, mini-units, extended research argument, and formative assessments, practicing K-16 teachers thought more deeply about how to create opportunities for critical discourse for their students.

Upon conclusion of this professional development, the two facilitators, a pre-service and graduate English methods professor at a large public university in the southeastern United States and an eighth-grade English language arts teacher (Steve) collaborated to implement the program with students attending a high needs public middle school by integrating it into the school's newly developed eighth-grade curriculum called the Responsible Change Project (RCP). Together, they developed a curriculum that combined elements of C3WP and critical service-learning to move young adolescent students to inquiry and social action. Utilizing a programmatic framework from the NWP's C3WP (NWP, 2015), Steve engaged his eighth-grade students in lessons, activities, and unit plans, modeling how to ask important questions related to the communities in which they lived. After observing in their communities, students honed their questions, conducted research into the root causes of and perspectives involved in the community issues, and then developed social action plans to address them. In many cases, Steve's eighth-grade students actually carried out their plans; they wrote, rehearsed, and delivered a TED-style talk to their classmates to inform and argue for a need to take action.

In this paper, we argue that by moving critical service-learning from the margins of curriculum and pedagogy into the foundation of planning, Steve fostered critical thinking and social action with students around issues of importance within their communities. This study examines the experience of one middle school English language arts teacher committed to empowering students to critically inquire into their communities and find voice around issues of social justice. The authors sought to answer the following research questions: (1) How did the combination of C3WP and RCP influence student growth in the intersections of literacy, engagement, and writing? (2) In what ways do middle grades students engage in research and service-learning to foster inquiry and develop their own solutions?

Context

Young adolescents in the United States identify a host of issues and concerns that mirror their parents and older generations. As a result of recent social and economic policies that affect the potential for the success of today's youth, it has become the mission of justice-oriented educators (Butin, 2003; Conklin & Hughes, 2016) to advocate for students in ways that show them their value and the promise they hold for our future. For example, the expanding wage gap in the southern states has resulted in an increase in the numbers of youth living in poverty. In a widely reported recent Harvard-Berkeley study, the city closest to the town where we conducted our research ranked 50th out of the 50 largest US cities and 97th of the 100 largest US cities for economic mobility (Chetty, Hendren, Kline, & Saez, 2014). To provide more specific context, in 2016, the governor approved the controversial HB2 law preventing transgender kids from using the restrooms in which they feel most comfortable while at school. Further, the murder and incarceration rate of young African American males has consistently increased over all other racial groups year after year. Finally, since the 2016 election, increased ICE (Immigration and Customs Enforcement) raids and the termination of DACA (Bruno, 2017) have raised awareness and terror among undocumented student populations across the state. All in all, the rights of marginalized populations are under assault in this state and across the country. This negativity prompted Steve and his colleagues to consider ways in which they might challenge middle school students to identify causes of concern in their communities and encourage them to conduct research around ways to promote positive change. Thus, they developed a curriculum to foster social justice through service-learning, critical literacy, and inquiry—this became the RCP.

Engendering a Social Justice Perspective

According to Brameld (2000), "Education has two major roles: to transmit culture and to modify culture. When American culture is in a state of crisis, the second of these roles—that of modifying and innovating—becomes more important" (p. 75). To educators dedicated to social justice, the goal of teaching becomes promoting equity and helping students to understand the relationship between power and oppression (Matteson & Boyd, 2017). By combining critical service-learning with deep, critical reflective reading of texts, or critical literacy, teachers can challenge students to engage in social action to improve conditions for their communities.

Service-learning, a type of pedagogy that combines community service and intentional content connected to academic learning goals, has long been identified as a promising practice for middle school classrooms (Kaye, 2010; Wilhelm, 2009). In 2009, Wilhelm suggested that a curriculum based in service-learning has the potential for engaging middle school students in authentic learning and developing students as change agents. In fact, Wilhelm (2009) recommended that every school implement service-learning across the content areas. Further, Glickman and Thompson (2009) argued for the importance of adding service-learning into the middle school curriculum, citing a moment where teachers must push back against standardization. They provide detailed steps for teachers hoping to implement a service-learning curriculum using the Preparation, Action, Reflection, and Celebration (PARC) Model (RMC, 2009). This method of service-learning follows the traditional expectations of planning, acting, and reflecting, while also enabling middle school students to celebrate or share their work as a demonstration to the community.

Mitchell (2008) differentiated critical service-learning from the traditional model of service-learning, suggesting that more traditional methods of service-learning assume that social justice is already present in the teaching of skills and content, whereas *critical* service-learning requires instructors to incorporate activities and reflections that motivate a social change orientation, engage students in examination of redistribution of power, and develop authentic relationships. As such, students participating in critical service-learning must learn to view themselves as agents of social change and "use the experience of service to address and respond to injustice in communities" (p. 51) (see Figure 1.1).

Similarly, Hart (2006) defines critical service-learning as "rooted in the aim of connecting academic instruction to the social, political, and economic conditions of students' lived experiences" (p. 18).

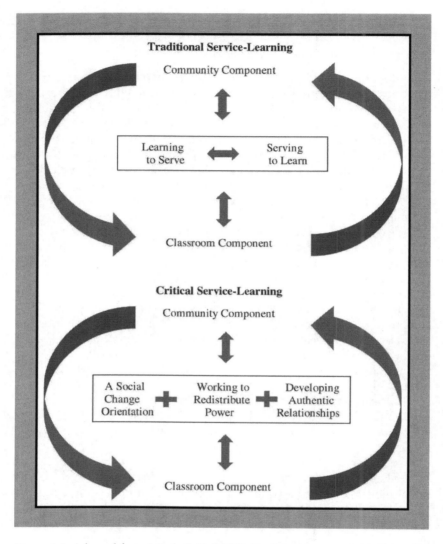

Figure 1.1 Adapted from Mitchell, T. (2008). Traditional versus Critical Service-Learning: Engaging the Literature to Differentiate Two Models

Source: Michigan Journal of Community Service Learning, 14(2), 50–65, under the Creative Commons Attribution License

When integrating a critical service-learning pedagogy into an English language arts course, teachers have a perfect opportunity to develop critical literacy with their students. Butler (2017) explained, "where and how young people engage in acts of being, speaking, reading, writing, and meaning-making are intricately connected to these young people's lives and livelihood" (p. 84). More specifically, teachers dedicated to this type of liberatory pedagogy (Freire, 1970) find ways to develop critical literacy with students through promoting inquiry into community issues and making connections to course content. By critiquing texts of all mediums for themes of power (Luke, 2000), learners unmask inequity and begin to act for social change. While engaging in this study, we noticed that the intersections of critical service-learning and critical literacy give life to a social justice perspective.

The Responsible Change Project

Over the course of an academic semester, Steve led his eighth-grade English language arts students in activities designed to challenge them to think about concerns within their communities. Focused on social justice inquiry, research, informal and formal research-based writing, service-learning, and TED-talk style presentations, Steve facilitated a curriculum that also included discussion and reflection along the way. As students began to conduct research into their topics on a larger scale, they consulted primary documents, informational texts, and even social media to gauge the degree to which their concerns were related to the national conversation on the topic.

The level of research, analysis, and writing that Steve expected from his students throughout this project required several high-level skills as a continuation of instruction from the first semester during the implementation of the early assignments in the NWP's C3WP curriculum. This program focused students' attention on different aspects of argument writing that drew on informational texts as sources. Early in the year, for example, students worked on developing a claim in response to reading several texts on immigration. At another time, while reading texts about the subject of reality television, students created a piece of writing that not only made a clear claim but also selected appropriate evidence from the text to support that claim and develop an argument. Other skills students learned during the first semester included commenting on and integrating source material into their writing, developing a clear line of reasoning, and addressing opposing viewpoints. This sustained and recursive exposure to developing an argument prepared Steve's students to apply the skills they learned in the close-reading and argument writing that the RCP asked of them.

The authors originally engaged in this work to test the potential of the C3WP curriculum for engaging middle school students in developing writing and communication skills around the state's English language arts curriculum. While providing space for developing curricular skills around topics of interest, Steve enabled students to develop a deeper connection with these topics and with the community in which they lived.

In what follows, we explain how students developed critical literacy, engaged in social and political discussions, and improved their writing and communication skills.

Methodology

The authors conducted this exploratory case study as a pilot study to determine the potential outcomes of coupling the C3WP curriculum with the RCP. Over the course of one semester, the first author observed and participated in planning sessions with Steve as he implemented the RCP. The authors sought to determine the potential for combining C3WP curriculum with critical literacy and service-learning to promote a social justice perspective. In this pilot study, Steve tested the curriculum so that the school could implement it on a larger scale with the entire eighth grade the following year. At the time of the study, Steve, a white male, had been teaching eighth-grade English language arts in this ethnically and socioeconomically diverse Title I middle school for 14 years. Students' self-identification of their ethnicity included 45% white students, 31% black students, 19% Hispanic students, 2% Asian students, and 3% students who identified with two or more races. In regard to socioeconomic status demographics, approximately 65% of students were eligible for free lunch, 20% of students were eligible for reduced lunch, and 15% of students were ineligible for free or reduced lunch.

Using participatory action research (Kemmis, 2006), a form of qualitative research methods, the authors analyzed the data through iterative coding and triangulated with member checking and co-authorship. This process enabled the identification of themes related to the guiding research questions and confirmed the validity of the processes (Yin, 2009). We analyzed data from this study in the form of teacher observations and both formal and informal interviews for themes related to social justice. The principle source of data within this study included transcripts of interviews with Steve. Interview questions focused on the ways in which this type of pedagogy might fit with the pedagogy mandated by state and local districts.

Findings from the data analysis describe Steve's process for engaging this group of eighth-grade students in inquiry-based learning that facilitated an understanding of social justice, both as an individual concept and as a goal for society. Additionally, Steve's responses to interview questions demonstrate the ways in which he grappled with the process and how he felt students grew in response to the challenge.

Mapping the Process

There were several entry points into the work of the RCP. The first occurred well before the project officially began in January. In the fall, in conjunction with NWP initiatives such as "Letters to the Next President" and mini-units from C3WP (NWP, 2016), students were exposed to a variety of social justice issues that were happening around the country, such as police use of force, race relations, poverty, and immigration policy. Through many heated class discussions, students also learned more about the multiple perspectives connected to those issues. This learning took place through a recursive series of lessons that focused on reading informational texts, developing nuanced claims, connecting claims to evidence, and developing written arguments that comment on material from multiple sources. This process developed a classroom culture of argument, where students learned to listen, consider different viewpoints, and ask critical questions or engage in discourse, in addition to learning about argument writing and current events. Many of the topics that students discussed during this first part of the year would end up planting the seeds of ideas for their RCP topics. This time was also important for the creation of Steve's class community and establishing a culture of civil discourse. Without building both this knowledge base and classroom culture, the RCP would not have been nearly as deep and thoughtful.

In the brainstorming stages of this project, students identified issues within their communities that were of concern to them. By the end of the semester, once students conducted their research and created their action plans, there were 69 different topics identified by 140 students. Although many of these concerns spanned a wide variety of topics, students reduced and combined the most commonly identified concerns to include the following: gun violence ($N = 21$), bullying ($N = 15$), hunger/poverty ($N = 9$), alcohol and drug abuse ($N = 9$), and human trafficking ($N = 8$). Other topics that students identified included domestic violence, teen pregnancy, animal cruelty, racism, suicide, and Post-Traumatic Stress Disorder.

A quick review of student concerns indicated that young adolescents think about the same types of issues that adults consider on a daily basis. Steve hypothesized that the large number of students interested in researching and creating an action plan related to gun violence was a direct response to the shooting death of a classmate in January. Furthermore, middle school students often identify bullying as a topic of concern to them. As this is a Title I middle school, it was not surprising that a large number of students identified hunger and poverty as major concerns within their communities. Although it might seem strange for middle school students to be concerned about human trafficking, the state in which this study took place is consistently ranked in the top ten states for cases of human trafficking. In fact, the state saw a 62% increase in cases of human trafficking in 2016 (National Human Trafficking Hotline, 2017).

Developing Critical Literacy

Upon identification of the topics that concerned them, students engaged in formal research and writing, a process that took about three weeks. Most students started their research on the Internet, seeking out credible sources of information on the underlying causes of the issues and the current and historical state of it in the country. During the planning stages of the project, Steve explained that "being able to critically evaluate content was of particular importance at a time where most information found on social topics was highly polarized and in some cases fabricated." Therefore, both before and while students did their research, Steve led them in several assignments focused on evaluating web information. Using the Currency, Reliability, Author/Authority, and Purpose/Point-of-View approach (Blakesee, 2010), Steve's students examined and discussed a collection of websites. While some of the sites were intentionally misleading (fake news), others were either explicitly biased or more subtly supporting a particular interest.

Steve clarified, "This exercise in analysis taught students to ask questions about the sources they found online and not take information at face value." Steve emphasized to students how finding a source that expressed a biased perspective did not necessarily disqualify it from being a source for their research; they just needed to be aware of that bias and seek out information that collectively represented the diverse positions of their subject. As he modeled the research process to students (forming questions, finding and analyzing sources, taking and organizing notes, writing), Steve used the example topic of "fake news" to serve the dual purpose of demonstration and reinforcement of the importance in evaluating website credibility.

Students combed through current events articles, opinion/editorials, and videos, using the web tool Diigo to annotate and organize their findings. With this background understanding, students conducted their own primary research by creating and implementing surveys and interviews. Students synthesized all this information into a research report that included an introduction to the topic and why it was important to the student and community, drew conclusions based on the information from the research sources (a claim supported by evidence), and made recommendations for further action. These recommendations served as a starting place for the next part of the project, where students fleshed out what they would do to create change.

Gaining Agency

When asked about how he felt about the process of beginning this work, Steve explained that guiding students through the RCP was neither easy nor neat. In fact, he admitted that engaging in this project was completely exhausting.

Every group of students was doing something different; each had unique problems they were trying to work through and often didn't have quite all of the skills or knowledge they needed to accomplish the big tasks they were setting out to do.

When questioned about the social skills that students developed through this experience, Steve identified skills such as formatting and sending an e-mail, asking for donations, finding the appropriate contact in cases where permission was required, approaching and accepting rejection, and considering the needs of a particular audience. Throughout this six-month period, these were all skills Steve found himself teaching individuals and groups as students were working through the process of carrying out their plans. Despite the hectic and uncontrollable nature of this work in the beginning stages, Steve realized that students had not just developed additional knowledge, "they also gained the agency that comes with taking the initiative and doing something that matters in the world." This energy drove the latter stages of the work.

Steve also drew upon students' deepened knowledge and new-found passion for creating and delivering speeches. Over several weeks, students watched and analyzed several TED talks—persuasive presentations where speakers discussed innovative ideas around topics about which they were passionate. In many of the TED talks, students saw that speakers were knowledgeable and passionate not just because they conducted research or took a class, but because they were in some way personally connected to the subject about which they were speaking. Steve guided students as they watched these videos and read the accompanying transcripts to identify and analyze the important parts and what made them work.

Steve noted, "These talks were the models students turned to as they began to prepare their own presentations that would take an audience through the process of learning and activism." The presentations lasted a week, with each student or group of students standing before an audience of their classmates, interested teachers, and members of the community. Although each only lasted three to five minutes, all students told a story of learning and activism, each conveying an impressive scope of the transformative work that motivated and supported what young adolescents can do. Steve explained:

> These presentations were the most powerful arguments students created throughout the year. It wasn't just that students by this point had a strong command of writing a source-based argument focused around a claim. It was because that through their action, they developed agency and investment. They carved out place in the complex conversation around their topic, and with confidence and passion, felt a personal reason to bring others in with them. For me, it further

validated the action piece of the project, highlighting the connection between doing real-world work and crafting arguments that are truly authentic.

At the end of the year, after the implementation of RCP, Steve noted that many students explained how this project was the most meaningful thing they did in school all year. In an e-mail communication at the end of the school year, Steve wrote:

> So much happened from start to finish which students found value in. Even if in the midst of the experience, that value was not fully realized. In the end, the general consensus was that this project was challenging and worthwhile.

Along the way, there were some challenges. The responsibility placed on students to be change-makers came with uncertainty and confusion. However, Steve explained that this work was valuable to the development of students' sense of agency.

Developing Skills of Inquiry and Empathy and Engendering a Social-Justice Mindset

Through RCP, students learned important skills such as asking critical questions and thinking beyond themselves. Steve described the development of these skills as being "more than I could have taught them through a book study." He went on to say:

> The questioning skill is one that is developed through taking the open-ended inquiry stance. Students learned first-hand the impact that questioning has on their own learning. The more experience students had with this approach, the better they became at not just finding answers to their questions, but also asking new questions which then guided subsequent learning.

Over the course of the semester, students also learned to think beyond themselves. With each topic researched or discussed, students began with their own experiences and reactions. By focusing on their own interests, students invested in their own experience and found answers to help or speak to the community around them. Steve noticed students were listening carefully to their classmates:

> As students learned to develop their own claims, they did so through a process that involved sharing and receiving responses from classmates. Often, these quick response sessions led to the discussions that prompted student revisions—clarification of a point they wanted to

make, removal of a point that wasn't relevant, or even a change of the positions that was initially taken. It was a process that revealed the importance of listening and highlighted the value of ideas and experiences of others.

Students learned to see that there were multiple "correct" and informed ways to look at the world and that positions others took could inform students' own evolving understandings. Steve explained, "When this happens, again and again, a classroom community evolves that is more open and empathetic, one where all have an appreciation for how knowledge is socially situated."

As students asked questions about their topics and began the process of researching, they, of course, learned plenty of background about the issue. This broad background knowledge was important and likely necessary for what students learned about how their topic operated in the world. Most students began their inquiry with an oversimplified understanding of their issue. However, as inquiry continued, students' questions led to new questions. When students encountered views different from their own, and when they interacted with those in the community directly affected by the issue, students acquired a more nuanced understanding of both their subject and how the greater society connected to the issue. In this way, Steve argued that students developed cultural capital, which is the set of skills and understandings a person develops over time for social promotion (Bourdieu, 1984). Through this project, these young adolescents learned to challenge their peers and themselves while also examining the reproduction of social norms.

Measuring Outcomes

It is important to point out that this project was designed with the expectation that measurement would not be driving the work, but that Steve would assess student progress formatively. Steve analyzed how students used sources in argument writing, responded to written reflections, and assessed presentation skills and participation. He collected and analyzed student writing samples for argument development with the C3WP "Using Sources Tool," which measures a student's ability to integrate sources into a piece of writing in a way that supports the development of an argument. Steve also examined the ways in which students used the sources to guide the reader to the writer's perspective (i.e., authorizing, illustrating, extending, countering (Harris, 2006)).

Steve did not select an assessment method prior to creating the assignment, as he wanted to provide students with the opportunity to choose their own form of activism. However, the TED-talk style speeches that students delivered at the culminating event provided the mode for skillful use of sources in carefully crafted arguments. Steve reflected, "We could have measured the use of argument strategies in the presentations; this type of measurement would be useful for the next iteration of the project." The TED-talks students composed and delivered were some of the most exciting source-based arguments students created all year. Composed of personal stories, experiences with the project, research findings, visual aids, and even some performance poetry, these pieces were arguments that were complex and highly personal—a feature strengthened by the voices students used to tell them.

Confronting Challenges in Service-Learning Pedagogy

Often when projects come to an end, teachers want to tell success stories, creating a narrative marked by student work that is polished and significant, pointing to examples of what students accomplished and illustrating the importance and scope of the grade-level curriculum. In the case of the RCP, such a highlight reel would center around one group's presentation on pet safety at a local elementary school and another's community cookout. These projects made a strong claim for students participating in critical service-learning as part of a traditional school curriculum. Although many of the individuals and groups desired to provide more direct service, these two groups exemplified the implementation of successful, large-scale projects. By providing a short presentation to elementary school students, one group hoped to prevent animal cruelty. The other group planned and executed a powerful moment for the community to come together to heal after the loss of a classmate, a community cookout featured in the local newspapers and broadcast on the local television news.

Recognition That Advocacy Work Is Difficult

Focusing solely on success stories, though, misrepresents the experiences of many other groups of students—those who struggled to ever find direction, who became overwhelmed by all the problems they encountered, or could not quite pull off what they had planned. Engaging students in critical service-learning is an exciting prospect for a school project, but that shiny excitement quickly dulls when students have the responsibility to take ownership of their learning. Steve explained:

> In several cases, eighth graders struggled to complete the work of enacting their plans for creating change; many students did not know where to start. Others started out with a full head of steam, but quickly became deflated when they realized what they wanted to do was not going to work as they envisioned. Classroom activity moved at a furious pace initially—plans being started, abandoned, revised—it was

impossible to really get a feel on any sense of direction. No one had a frame of reference for the work we were doing.

This was both the students' and teacher's first experience with this sort of civic engagement in school. At times, students felt lost, and so did Steve.

Upon conclusion of the project, Steve reflected, "The initial part of making the action piece happen was the most wobbly for both the students and me. I was asking them to engage with the community, but they didn't know how." As an example, one group had an idea to host an event for the community at a local park, but they became frustrated at not knowing how to turn this idea into action. They did not know where to start or what logistically their project would entail. Of course, Steve and their parents supported them along the way, but there were plenty of moments where all involved felt incredibly overwhelmed. Students also experienced a lot of frustration when they ran into unforeseen obstacles in carrying out their plans. After the community cookout occurred, Steve reflected in an e-mail:

> As adults, we know that things don't always work, and problem-solving is a part of any project process, but students were so used to just following the pathway set for them in school to a neat end that they weren't equipped to address the messiness of the pathway or the end when it was presented. Guiding students through problems was teaching them a critically important civics skill. In the end, many students had a strong sense of accomplishment through working through this iterative process, but there were also other students who left the experience with their project derailed and feeling frustrated.

Despite the initial confusion, both Steve and his students sorted out their ideas and proceeded slowly, but still with excitement. From the uncertainty emerged student voice, empowerment, and knowledge to support student questions and potential solutions. Steve admitted that he "found a new sort of value in my students and recognized the importance of encouraging them to seek out innovative approaches to disseminating their research and posing their solutions to the community."

Recommendations for Teachers Hoping to Engage in Similar Work

This work was a massive undertaking. However, when spread throughout a semester and connected to standards, it was an endeavor that Steve was empowered to do. Steve described the RCP as "an opportunity to engage students civically." Because he developed it as part of the eighth-grade curriculum, he did not have to rush through it due to the need to get back to the content and curriculum. At the end of the school year, Steve reflected:

> This project provided the time and an appropriate progression to really get students to dig in with the questions they had, take action, and engage with an authentic and interested audience. In the coming iteration of the project, ELA teachers on different wings of the school will collaborate on this work as part of their professional learning community. Despite not knowing what this effort will look like, we will plan it as collaboratively as possible and have the opportunity to reflect, revise, and re-plan with your support.

Members of the NWP site applied and successfully received another round of SEED grant funding to expand the C3WP curriculum throughout all ELA classrooms in the school and to support the RCP project with all eighth-grade ELA teachers. This funding not only provided a stipend for ELA teachers to attend a three-day professional development session around C3WP, but also funded a team of teacher consultants from the Writing Project site as mentors.

The framework, timeline, and vision for first year of the collaboration between students served as a model for the following year for whole-grade implementation. Steve explained that in addition to developing an understanding of what works, "I also got a sense of what didn't work—mainly any student project that was created with the hopes of raising funds within the school or that would disrupt the school day." Thus, teachers avoided those projects in the second year, and reworked the action component of the project to include a more direct service-orientation. Overall, the learning that happened over the course of the initial year through this project was encouraging and served as a powerful model for the subsequent year (for which we are now analyzing data).

Significance

Steve views literacy as a vehicle through which children can learn about and act on the world. Schools often put emphasis on the first part and just hope that the latter part happens outside of school or later in life. This is unfortunate for a couple of reasons. First, a task of schools is to prepare students for life in a democracy, which requires that educators inform and empower students as active participants in the world. To participate in society, people need to understand agency and have some knowledge of how the civic participation process works. There is not a light switch that people can just turn on; justice-oriented teaching requires guiding students in taking part in society through the messy, real-world, authentic experiences connected to their interests (Coffey, Fitchett, & Farinde, 2015; Conklin, 2008; Conklin & Hughes, 2016). This is how students learn agency. It is also what provides relevance to the reading and writing that teachers must ask students to do.

When teachers ask students to engage in literacy because we tell them they "have to" or to earn a certain grade, the purpose for literacy is ours (teachers, schools), not theirs. And while there are times when this sort of instruction ought to happen, it cannot be the only way. Through our experience with the students in this study, we learned that students develop as literate beings who value and see the purpose of reading, writing, speaking, and listening when they can use those literate practices for their own self-interests and with the purpose of enacting change. That is why the critical service-learning and critical literacy part must be present in order for students to become agents for social change. We propose that when students seek out and create connections with the community, this connectedness provides context for literacy learning that is student driven, rather than teacher-assigned, as well as relevant and powerful.

Now, more than ever, we need research that shows practical applications of the importance of how social contexts matter in teaching, learning, student growth, and in the development of equitable and just forms and systems of education. This project contributes to the body of research describing the ways in which we might demand better educational experiences for our children around the world. We currently face the startling growth in income disparity in the United States, and like our children, youth around the world consistently confront racial, ethnic, sexual, gender, linguistic, and social class inequalities across local, national, and global contexts. Furthermore, the disparate access to information requires that as teachers, we demonstrate for youth how to analyze the texts they encounter on a daily basis for messages of power and privilege. We must show them how to determine whether they are represented appropriately and how to assess whether others are as well.

Teachers are de-professionalized daily by inequitable accountability measures, prescribed curriculum, and practices they know are not research based. This study presents findings from a teacher who decided to act in the best interest of his students by engaging them in critical service-learning pedagogy that examines the structural causes of inequity within their communities. Through this project, students became informed, developed writing, reading, and research skills, and gained a sense of empowerment when given the opportunity to ask questions that truly address issues within their lives.

Conclusion

This participatory action research (Kemmis, 2006) has implications for both teacher educators hoping to demonstrate teaching methods that foster liberatory, critical pedagogy for pre-service teachers and for practicing teachers who may be hesitant to engage in this type of pedagogy without a model. This paper presents specific activities and lessons used to facilitate the development of critical literacy with eighth-grade students from high poverty backgrounds and the outcomes from their own engagement in critical service-learning. Engaging culturally diverse students living in high-poverty areas in critical service-learning pedagogy can offer the opportunity to engage in the kind of inquiry that is important to the progress of their communities and help them understand the importance of social justice. Further, by offering teachers' guidelines and a curriculum that might work for their students, they might find autonomy in their classrooms once again.

References

Blakesee, S. (2010). *Currency, Relevance, Authority, Accuracy, Point of View (CRAAP)*. Meriam Library. Chicago: California State University. Retrieved from www.csuchico.edu/lins/handouts/eval_websites.pdf

Bourdieu, P. (1984). *Distinction: A social critique of the judgment of taste*. Cambridge, MA: Harvard University Press.

Brameld, T. (2000). *Education as power*. San Francisco, CA: Caddo Gap Press.

Bruno, A. (2017). *Deferred action for childhood arrivals*. Congressional Research Service. Retrieved from https://fas. org/sgp/crs/homesec/R44764.pdf

Butin, D. W. (2003). Of what use is it? Multiple conceptualizations of service learning within education. *Teachers College Record*, *105*(9), 1674–1692. https://doi.org/10.1046/j.1467-9620.2003.00305.x

Butler, T. (2017). "We need a song": Sustaining critical youth organizing literacies through world humanities. *Equity & Excellence in Education*, *50*(1), 84–95. https://doi.org/10.1080/10665684.2016.1250233

Chetty, R., Hendren, N., Kline, P., & Saez, E. (2014). Where is the land of opportunity: The geography of intergenerational mobility in the United States. *Quarterly Journal of Economics*, *129*(4), 1553–1623. https://doi.org/10.1093/qje/qju022

Coffey, H. M., Fitchett, P. G., & Farinde, A. A. (2015). It takes courage: Fostering the development of critical, social justice-oriented teachers using museum and project-based instruction. *Action in Teacher Education*, *37*(1), 9–22. https://doi.org/10.1080/01626620.2014.971136

Conklin, H. G. (2008). Modeling compassion in critical, justice-oriented teacher education. *Harvard Educational Review*, *78*(4), 652–674. https://doi.org/10.17763/haer.78.4.j80j17683q870564

Conklin, H. G., & Hughes, H. (2016). Practices of compassionate, critical, justice-oriented teacher education. *Journal of Teacher Education*, *67*(1), 47–60. https://doi.org/10.1177/0022487115607346

Freire, P. (1970). *Pedagogy of the oppressed*. New York: Continuum.

Glickman, C., & Thompson, K. (2009). Tipping the tipping point: Public engagement, education, and service-learning. *Voices from the Middle*, *17*(1), 9–15.

Harris, J. (2006). *Rewriting: How to do things with texts*. Logan, UT: University Press of Colorado. Retrieved from www.jstor.org/stable/j.ctt4cgnf2

Hart, S. (2006). Breaking literacy boundaries through critical service-learning: Education for the silenced and marginalized. *Mentoring & Tutoring: Partnership in Learning, 14*(1), 17–32. https://doi.org/10.1080/13611260500432236

Kaye, C. B. (2010). *The complete guide to service learning*. Minneapolis, MN: Free Spirit Publishing Inc.

Kemmis, S. (2006). Participatory action research and the public sphere. *Educational Action Research, 14*(4), 459–476. https://doi.org/10.1080/09650790600975593

Luke, A. (2000). Critical literacy in Australia. *Journal of Adolescent and Adult Literacy, 43*, 448–461.

Matteson, H., & Boyd, A. (2017). Are we making "PROGRESS"? A critical literacies framework to engage pre-service teachers for social justice. *Journal of Language & Literacy Education, 13*(1), 28.

Mitchell, T. (2008). Traditional vs. critical service-learning: Engaging the literature to differentiate two models. *Michigan Journal of Community Service Learning, 14*(2), 50–65.

National Human Trafficking Hotline. (2017, June 30). *North Carolina*. Retrieved from https://humantraffickinghotline.org/state/north-carolina

National Writing Project. (2015). *College, Career, and Community Writing Project (C3WP)*. Retrieved from https://sites.google.com/site/nwpcollegereadywriters program/home

National Writing Project. (2016). *Letters to the next president 2.0*. Retrieved from https://letters2president.org/

RMC Research Corporation. (2009). *K-12 service-learning project planning toolkit*. Scotts Valley, CA: National Service-Learning Clearinghouse.

Wilhelm, J. (2009). The audacity of service: Students as agents of possibility. *Voices From the Middle, 17*(1), 34–37.

Yin, R. K. (2009). *Case study research: Design and methods*. Thousand Oaks, CA: Sage Publications.

2 Middle School Curriculum Aimed at Developing Agents of Change

Michelle Rupenthal and Shelly Furuness

This We Believe Characteristics

- Curriculum is challenging, exploratory, integrative, and relevant.
- Educators value young adolescents and are prepared to teach them.
- Organizational structures foster purposeful learning and meaningful relationships.

Leadership and Organization

Designing curricular experiences that meet both the philosophical spirit and the academic demands of excellent middle grades education is never an easy task, but it is possible when there is a clear vision and strong commitment from teachers and administrative leaders in a building. In 1990 and again in 2005, James Beane articulated a clear vision and process for moving a middle school curriculum from rhetoric to reality. In Beane's (2005) vision, the most important purpose of schools is "to help our students learn the democratic way of living" (p. 1). John Lounsbury (1990) wondered in the foreword of Beane's pioneering text on middle-level curriculum, "[H]ave we the vision, the commitment, the courage, the initiative, and the patience to do the thorough rebuilding of school programs that is needed?" (p. vi). What follows is a description of a language arts curriculum inspired by those questions raised in Beane's seminal work and by his subsequent call to democratic, hopeful teaching "with its curriculum based on real-life situations and projects" (Beane, 2005, p. 7). Supporting this description is the story of one teacher's attempt to implement a curriculum inspired by Beane's foundational vision that would answer Lounsbury's questions in the affirmative and blur the walls between school life and civic life by making space for student voice.

Noblesville East is the smaller of two suburban middle schools in the heart of a Midwestern school district. It has approximately 1,144 students. Seventy-eight percent of the students are white and 35% receive free or reduced lunch and textbook support. Guided by the Association for Middle-Level Education (formerly National Middle School Association) 16 key characteristics of successful middle grades schools as outlined in *This We Believe* (2010), Noblesville East's principal leads his faculty in creating a responsive school climate by empowering teachers to be curricular and instructional leaders. That commitment began with staffing East with educators who value young adolescents and are prepared to teach them (NMSA, 2010). In part, East's mission is to provide a "comprehensive, responsive, and effective program designed to meet the unique academic and social needs of middle school students" (Noblesville East Middle School, n.d., About Us section, "Middle School Program Guide"). Two structures within the school, interdisciplinary teaming and discipline-specific professional learning communities (PLCs), support this mission. The teachers within an interdisciplinary team focus their work on meeting the social, emotional, and academic needs of their approximately 120 shared students while those same teachers also work within their discipline-specific PLCs to collaborate on the design of curriculum as well as instruction. It is within the context of a discipline-specific PLC that three eighth grade language arts teachers felt inspired to develop meaningful curriculum around "common needs, problems, interests, and concerns of young people and the society" (Beane, 1990, p. 35).

One of the eighth-grade language arts teachers discovered Beane's 1990 work in her own learning and shared his ideas with her PLC. Further professional learning led to the discovery of his 2005 text, *A Reason to Teach: Creating Classrooms of Dignity and Hope*. Given the political climate in which skills-based academic achievement is the primary focus and the structure of a school day which limits true interdisciplinary work across content area teachers, the language arts teachers looked for places where they could try to live into the spirit of Beane's call to action to create a real and relevant curriculum for real adolescents. The result was a curriculum that resonates with students as it blurred the walls between school life and civic life and gave more opportunities for student voice. The teachers recognized the power and possibility that exist for young adolescents in spaces Beane described as:

> The intersection of personal concerns and social issues . . . and [i]n the intersections between these two categories . . . [educators] discover a promising way of conceptualizing a general education that serves the dual purpose of addressing the personal issues, needs, and problems of early adolescents and the concerns of the larger world, including the particular society in which they live.
>
> (Beane, 1990, p. 40)

The educators at East took seriously "the intersection of personal concerns and social issues" (Beane, 1990, p. 41) as well as the "persistent concepts" (p. 43) that endure in the lives of early adolescents. While we acknowledge that the concept of middle school philosophy continues to be actively explored by passionate middle school advocates (Cameli, 2017; Coffey & Fulton, 2018; Davis, 2017; Hagerman & Porath, 2018; Lounsbury, 2017), it was the intentional investigation of Beane's seminal work that fueled the creation of this curriculum. These teachers acknowledged that institutional structures and state mandates often impose constraints upon fully realizing Beane's vision of a true middle school curriculum even in schools that are intentional in their vision. However, the PLC teachers simultaneously looked for a "way of bringing the content of democracy to the surface . . . in classrooms where teachers organize the curriculum around personally and socially significant themes" (Beane, 2005, p. 32). Working within the institutional structures and state mandates, the PLC teachers found ways to begin to bring Beane's ideals from rhetoric to reality.

Curriculum, Instruction, and Assessment

Using the foundational principles of Beane's vision for democratic curriculum, teachers within the PLC collaborated to create a year-long curriculum for their eighth-graders that was challenging, exploratory, integrative, and relevant (NMSA, 2010). The teachers adapted Beane's framework to develop "curriculum [that] treat[s] young people with dignity . . . [and] value[s] the knowledge and experience that young people bring with them to school, as well as the knowledge that they think would be worth pursuing" (Beane, 2005, p. 135). The teachers organized this year-long curriculum around four essential questions which align with Arnold's (as cited in Beane, 1990) insights on adolescent inquiries:

> Young adolescents are asking some of the most profound questions human beings can ever ask: Who am I? What can I be? What should I be? What should I do? To respond to them effectively, we must forge a curriculum that frequently deals with their own questions.
>
> (Beane, 1990, p. 37)

These questions moved students toward blurring the boundaries between school and civic life as they are rooted in the study of humanities rather than specific to the discipline of language arts. Each of those four questions became the frame for a unit of study, resulting in a year-long curriculum that had four quarter-long units which placed tremendous value on the personal concerns of the students, provided opportunities to engage the students in finding solutions to their own concerns, and encouraged students to become agents of change (NMSA, 2010).

Although three teachers collaborated to create this curriculum, what follows is how one of the teachers, in her third year of teaching, enacted it. The data comes from artifacts such as student work, lesson plans, and teacher and student reflections from the one teacher's five sections of eighth grade language arts, which include students with learning disabilities, English language arts learners, and high-ability students.

Unit One Question: Who Are We?

> Life is always reminding you when you are in tune with yourself and when you are not. . . . In the end, we all recognize our song. Just keep singing and you'll find your way home.
>
> (Some, 1999)

While the end goal of the year was to develop students' desires to be agents of change in their communities, the first step involved exploring the identities, interests, and passions of each individual in the classroom. Beginning the journey by looking inward helped students to develop a greater awareness of who they are and a stronger sense of confidence to express that identity, both of which served them in the classroom community and the communities beyond the walls of the school. Additionally, this first step provided the teacher with understandings to best tailor the curriculum to the needs of her learners.

Planning with this goal in mind, the teachers designed the culminating assessment for the first unit to be a memoir in response to the essential question *who are we?* Students' inquiries about who they are as individuals and who they are as a group drove the entire unit. To scaffold those inquiries, teachers created opportunities for students to put their own understandings of themselves into writing and deepen those understandings through reading a variety of both self-selected and common texts. For instance, on the first day of school, to begin the journey of looking inward, the teacher asked her students to create six-word memoirs. Based on the example "For sale: baby shoes, never worn," frequently attributed to Ernest Hemingway (Conan, 2010), the task of writing a six-word memoir allowed for a student to select strong diction to share his or her story with the classroom community. While students participated in this task as a means of exploring their own identities, it simultaneously acted as a lesson in empathy as students heard the stories of their peers.

A series of activities followed this multi-faceted first step to invite the students to inquire into who they are as individuals and use their own voices to share their findings. For instance, students produced a short video, complete with original film footage from their lives, in response to the question "what makes your heart beat?", as inspired by the YouTube video "What Makes Your Heart Beat?" by Darling Magazine (2014). Over time, students also read the text "Lifesong of a Child" (Some, 1999) and selected their personal "lifesongs" that best reflected their identities, sketched roadmaps of the moments in their lives that led them to where they are today, and created a "Soul Selfie" by designing a digital graphic that synthesized a self-taken image with the character traits that best describe them. Additionally, students analyzed characters in their self-selected independent reading books using the metaphor of an iceberg to explore the aspects of an individual hidden below the surface. While these activities may appear surface-level at first glance, the teacher purposefully designed them as scaffolds to grant each student the time and space to explore who he or she is and who others are. By focusing on identities and passions, both individually and collectively, the students were on their way to recognizing their own songs. Once the students recognize their songs, they can utilize those aspects of themselves as strengths to empathize with the songs and stories of all individuals they encounter and address the problems they see in their communities.

Unit Two Question: What Can We Be?

> We should ask that the curriculum treat young people with dignity, as real people who live in the real world and care about its condition and fate.
> (Beane, 2005, p. 135)

The second step toward developing students into agents of change involved questioning the potential that exists in societies and the roles individuals can play in building their societies. To accomplish this goal, the essential question that the teacher posed to students in the second unit was *what can we be?* Students explored this question as they read a variety of self-selected dystopian texts, wrote essays analyzing the themes developed in dystopian novels and how those themes compare to their own societies, and created documentaries to capture an answer to student-created questions developed from their thematic connections.

In this second unit, the teacher scaffolded student inquiry by providing them with more than 40 dystopian novels to choose from based on their interests, such as *The Hunger Games* (Collins, 2008), *1984* (Orwell, 1949), *Divergent* (Roth, 2011), and many more. These fictional social commentaries assisted students in questioning the world around them as the plots, settings, conflicts, character development, and themes of the novels encouraged them to wonder what if, if only, and if this goes on, just as Neil Gaiman questioned in the 2013 foreword of *Fahrenheit 451* (Bradbury, 2012). As the students interacted with these texts, they analyzed the utopian and dystopian elements of these fictional societies to unveil new perspectives related to the question *what can we be?* Simultaneously, students investigated the lessons, or themes, the authors developed across the dystopian novels and the ways those themes connect to the societies in which the students are members. The teacher provided supportive mini lessons on finding credible sources and providing strong evidence to justify one's thinking. As an outcome of this literary analysis, students shared their new understandings gained from their inquiries. Examples of findings include the challenges of building the perfect society and that societies, like mirrors, are reflections of the choices made by the individuals within the society.

To solidify and deepen understandings such as these, students synthesized their new understandings gained from their research into a collaborative documentary. Working with a small group of their peers, students worked through a series of steps to craft a thematic question that would serve as a guide in the documentary creation process. These steps included identifying existing themes from dystopian texts, selecting the theme they want to explore further, formulating their own essential questions in order to explore the selected theme further, and working together to select the question that was most interesting to them and their audience. This part of the unit led students to inquire about the messages the dystopian novels deliver about societies and the ways individuals can apply those lessons to their own worlds as they asked the following questions: *Why should power be distributed? How can we make our world a more utopian place? In what ways can American citizens embrace the freedoms that they have? How can we welcome knowledge from all perspectives?* As students asked critical questions of the world around them, they looked outside the walls of the school for possible answers. Students became very resourceful as they reached out to local politicians for interviews, gathered film footage at community events like a local women's march, and visited places in the community whose missions led them to making the world a better place. Compiling these experiences through the documentary format allowed students to creatively display possible answers to their questions and to deliver their message to a larger audience.

Throughout this unit, there was an evolution that began with students looking critically at fictional communities in comparison to the communities in which they live, but over time, developing a hopeful stance on what those communities could be. The hope developed throughout this unit planted the seed for students to become agents of change.

Unit Three Question: What Should We Be?

> "*There is no more powerful way to initiate a significant change than to convene a conversation*"
>
> (Wheatley, 2002, p. 22).

After exploring the potential that exists in societies and learning that utopian societies are challenging to attain, the teacher invited students to question the judgments and opinions present in their societies through the essential question *what should we be?* In this third unit, the ultimate goal was for students to voice their ideas and opinions to start conversations that matter. Carrying the understandings and experiences from the first two units into this new unit, students recognized early on that there is no single, clear-cut answer to the essential question *what should we be?* Knowing this, students had the space to state their own claims and utilize persuasive techniques to convince their audience in two formats: an argumentative essay and a debate with their peers.

The unit began by introducing students to the persuasive appeals of ethos, logos, and pathos as well as other elements of argumentation. Students dissected a variety of arguments found in nonfiction texts, including current events and historical documents, for their use of persuasive techniques before applying those strategies to their own arguments. For their initial written arguments, students had free range on the topic that they developed using the persuasive techniques, but they also received support in locating strong evidence for their topic through a mini lesson on finding credible sources. The students decided to use their voices to take a stand on a variety of issues, examples of which include animal cruelty, inequitable pay based on gender, genetically modified foods, and the amount of time dedicated to standardized testing. Such topics allowed students to engage in conversations that matter to them as well as practice crafting an argument prior to engaging in a larger debate among their peers.

Once students felt equipped with the skills to stand up for their beliefs by convincing others through the use of credible research, emotional appeals, and logical reasoning, they formed debate teams based on their topical interests and the strengths they displayed in their previous argumentative writing task. Students collaborated with their debate team to collect evidence in a shared Google Document—applying what they learned from earlier mini lessons—and to craft new arguments to deliver in the spoken format of a debate. Students were on teams of three or four debating against a group of the same size, and the debates lasted for an average of 30 minutes as each student played a specific role within the debate: opener, argument presenter, rebuttal presenter, or closer. As the audience listened to the arguments, they participated in a backchannel conversation using the tool "Today's Meet." This background conversation engaged audience members digitally as they shared their own thoughts related to the live debate occurring before them and continued to consider the essential question: *What should we be?*

Throughout this unit, students developed their ability to look critically at an argument presented and express their views in a convincing manner. By investigating the opinions of others and communicating their own belief systems, students discovered how they can use their voices to start conversations that matter in order to make our society a better place.

Unit Four Question: What Should We Do?

> *"This time, we do respond. This time, we intervene"*
> *(Wiesel, 1999, p. 4).*

Over the course of the school year, students explored who they are as individuals, what they could be as members of a society, and what they should be based on their beliefs and opinions. This process led students to discovering their own potential as well as identifying some of the obstacles and problems their societies face. With these experiences under their belts, the last unit welcomes students to synthesize their understandings thus far in response to the question *what should we do?* This final question provides the platform for students to take action on an issue they are passionate about and fulfill the yearlong goal of becoming agents of change.

To launch students into thinking about solving problems they see in society, each student selected a text related to the Holocaust, a time in history that brings to light many injustices. These texts provided concrete examples of people encountering extreme hardship as a result of the destructive beliefs and actions of others as well as moments where individuals worked to counteract that hardship to find light in the darkness. In addition to selecting texts that were right for them in terms of their interests and current reading abilities, students explored a variety of children's books about the Holocaust, read Elie Wiesel's (1999) speech titled "The Perils of Indifference," analyzed poetry about finding hope in challenging times, and selected other nonfiction texts to build their background knowledge on this genocide. As students read these texts, they constructed understandings related to how one person can make a difference in a society. Students shared the understandings built through their reading through weekly Socratic discussions to hear the understandings of their peers, to make connections across texts and to their societies, and to use their voices to speak on topics that blurred the walls between school and civic life.

Ultimately, these discussions culminated in students completing two projects to "be the change" in their societies: a version of the "Kindness Rocks" project that involved the entire eighth grade painting positive messages on rocks and hiding them around the community to be the light for those facing dark times and an independent project where each student developed and implemented an action plan to be the change in a manner that was meaningful to him or her. Some of the results from the independent projects include one student baking cookies to deliver to people who are homeless, another student organizing a school-wide fundraiser for a local domestic violence shelter, a boy who recently faced the major hardship of losing a parent reaching out to his neighbors to express his gratitude for helping him during his time of need, and a girl creating a video montage of diverse individuals from across the world singing Woody Guthrie's (1944) song "This Is Your Land" and sharing it on YouTube.

These four creative examples just scratch the surface of ways students used their understandings gained throughout the year to create solutions to the problems they witnessed and get involved in overcoming the road-blocks that exist in our societies. By the end of the year, the students truly were agents of change.

Conclusion: Culture and Community

This process of students becoming agents of change developed from a shared commitment among a group of eighth grade language arts teachers to develop a real and relevant curriculum for real adolescents. In other words, the teachers involved in this process sought to affirm that they did have the vision, the commitment, the courage, the initiative, and the patience to do the thorough and necessary rebuilding of school programs. This story captures the first year of enacting a new curriculum; the results of this adaptation have inspired this group of teachers to find ways to involve students in the curriculum—beyond the choice and reflection opportunities offered to them in this initial implementation of a teacher-created curriculum—as well as to break down the school structures that inhibit teachers from further blending the disciplines. This process was an incremental change toward imagining different ways of thinking and doing for the future.

Ultimately, what transpired as a result of the challenging, exploratory, integrative, and relevant curriculum was the creation of a community that meets the needs of its middle schoolers and empowers them to think critically about the cultures and communities around them and the role they can play in those societies. When reflecting on their experiences with this curriculum of empowerment, students shared the following:

- "I've learned to question myself on the choices I have made versus the choices I should make in the future to be the change in society, so I can positively impact the lives of others."
- "I have gained more of an open mind and view things from all perspectives now."
- "As a person, I have become much more compassionate towards those unlike me, patient in situations where I am not in control, and easy-going through obstacles I face."

"In this eighth grade year, I have acknowledged that I do have an inner inspiration that can be the light for someone's darkness. . . . I can be one to make a change in the world and makes differences."

As these students transition into high school, they carry with them developing mindsets and skill sets needed to address the hurdles of power, privilege, and oppression that communities face. Such understandings will serve them as they continue to wonder about what the world could and should be and the capabilities they have to influence the outcomes.

References

Beane, J. A. (1990). *A middle school curriculum: From rhetoric to reality*. Columbus, OH: National Middle School Association.

Beane, J. A. (2005). *A reason to teach: Creating classrooms of dignity and hope*. Portsmouth, NH: Heinemann.

Bradbury, R. (2012). *Fahrenheit 451*. New York: Simon and Schuster.

Cameli, S. (2017). Making middle school philosophy work: Philosophy vs. mindset. *AMLE Magazine, 5*(3), 6–8.

Coffey, H., & Fulton, S. (2018). The responsible change project: Building a justice-oriented curriculum through critical service-learning. *Middle School Journal, 49*(5), 16–25. https://doi.org/10.1080/00940771.2018.1509560

Collins, S. (2008). *The hunger games*. New York: Scholastic Press.

Conan, N. (Host). (2010). *Can you tell your life story in exactly six words*. [Radio broadcast episode]. Retrieved March 15, 2019 from www.npr.org/templates/story/story.php?storyId=123289019

Darling Magazine. (2014). *What makes your heart beat?* [Video File]. Retrieved March 15, 2019 from https://youtu.be/a9O0jIMfdNs

Davis, J. (2017). Making it work, making it meaningful: These elements of the middle school concept need attention and commitment. *AMLE Magazine, 5*(3), 13–15.

Guthrie, W. (1944). *This land is your land* [Recorded by Moses Asch]. On The Asch Recordings, Volume 1 [Recording]. New York, NY.

Hagerman, D., & Porath, S. (2018). The possibilities of teaching for, with, and about social justice in a public middle school. *Middle School Journal, 49*(5), 26–34. https://doi.org/10.1080/00940771.2018.1509561

Lounsbury, J. H. (1990). Foreword. In J. Beane (Ed.), *A middle school curriculum: From rhetoric to reality* (pp. vii–viii). Columbus, OH: National Middle School Association.

Lounsbury, J. H. (2017). Reflections on teaching and learning: Educators have a responsibility to guide the moral development of youth. *AMLE Magazine, 5*(3), 16–19.

National Middle School Association (NMSA). (2010). *This we believe: Keys to educating young adolescents*. Westerville, OH: NMSA.

Noblesville East Middle School. (n.d.). *Middle school program overview*. Retrieved March 15, 2019 from www.noblesvilleschools.org/domain/136

Orwell, G. (1949). *1984*. New York: Harcourt.

Roth, V. (2011). *Divergent*. New York: Harper Collins Children's Books.

Some, S. E. (1999). *Welcoming spirit home: Ancient African teachings to celebrate children and community*. Novato, CA: New World Library.

Wheatley, M. J. (2002). *Turning to one another: Simple conversations to restore hope to the future* (1st ed.). San Francisco, CA: Berrett-Koehler Publishers.

Wiesel, E. (1999). *The perils of indifference* [Video Transcript]. Retrieved March 15, 2019 from http://americanrhetoric.com/speeches/ewieselperilsofindifference.html

3   An Intervention to Support Mathematics Self-Efficacy in Middle School

Lia D. Falco

This We Believe Characteristics

- Educators value young adolescents and are prepared to teach them.
- Curriculum is challenging, exploratory, integrative, and relevant.

Anyone who has spent time in a middle school classroom has likely heard students say, "I'm just not good at math", or "math is boring." In the moment, teachers may respond with a quick sentiment to the contrary or a pat, "Of course you're good at (or in) math." Yet, this type of exchange reveals something important about students' attitudes toward math that often emerges during middle school. As students enter the middle school years, important changes occur in their interests, motivation, self-concept, self-efficacy, and achievement (Jacobs, Lanza, Osgood, Eccles, & Wigfield, 2002). These changes often manifest as negative attitudes and declines in competence-beliefs, and this is particularly true for girls, especially within the domain of mathematics (Midgley, Feldlaufer, & Eccles, 1989). Declines in competence beliefs are concerning because they have important implications for student achievement and future decision-making (Skaalvik, Federici, & Klassen, 2015).

In the past several decades, there has been increasing emphasis on the importance of Science, Technology, Engineering, and Math (STEM)-related fields to the US economy. However, the number of students choosing to pursue STEM-related college degrees and occupations is declining (National Academy of Science, 2007; National Center for Education Statistics [NCES], 2012, 2016). In the US, white and Asian males predominantly hold STEM occupations (American Association of University Women [AAUW], 2010; National Science Foundation [NSF], 2015). Despite recent increases, females continue to be under-represented in math, physical science, and engineering-related fields. Women who hold degrees in science and engineering are less likely than men with similar degrees to be employed in these fields, constituting 23% of the science and engineering labor force and only 10% of employed physicists (NSF, 2015). Researchers attribute this largely to a lack of self-confidence in STEM subjects, low STEM career self-efficacy, and lack of social support and encouragement to pursue STEM-related educational and occupational aspirations (Franklin, 2013; Grossman & Porche, 2014; Shoffner, Newsome, Barrio Minton, & Wachter-Morris, 2015).

In response to concern over recruitment and retention of students in the STEM work force, many researchers and educators have worked to develop and implement interventions aimed at engaging high school students in STEM learning. The ultimate goal of such efforts is to influence students' career trajectories and achieve a strong and diverse STEM workforce. However, by the time students reach high school, they may have already made important decisions regarding their possible STEM preparation and participation (Tai, Liu, Maltese, & Fan, 2006). Therefore, it is critical that educational programs and practices intended to improve STEM access and engagement begin as early as middle school to influence students' educational and career aspirations effectively. For girls, a self-efficacy intervention in middle school may be pivotal in terms of their future educational and career trajectory.

Self-efficacy refers to individuals' perceptions about their capabilities for learning or performing tasks within specific domains. Since Bandura (1977, 1997) introduced the construct of self-efficacy, researchers have explored its role in various contexts including career development. In social cognitive theory, self-efficacy influences behaviors and environments and, in turn, is influenced by them (Bandura, 1986, 1997). Students with strong self-efficacy are more likely to set goals and create adaptive learning environments for themselves. Hackett and Betz (1981) first used self-efficacy theory, within a career development context, to explain women's avoidance of math and science careers. Self-efficacy tenets (Bandura, 1986) now explain, more broadly, individuals' vocational behaviors. Within the social-cognitive framework, level of self-efficacy is one critical factor for predicting female and other under-represented minority students' engagement and persistence in the STEM pipeline (Chemers, Zurbriggen, Syed, Goza, & Bearman, 2011; Grossman & Porche, 2014). The outcomes that young people anticipate in considering a STEM career are closely connected to their self-efficacy beliefs in math (Falk, Rottinghaus, Casanova, Borgen, & Betz, 2017).

Middle School, Mathematics Self-Efficacy, and STEM

Adolescence is a critical time during development when students are exploring and acquiring academic and career-related interests as well as attitudes and self-beliefs related to their competence in different academic subjects.

By the time students reach middle school (grades six through eight), the majority have already determined significant preferences toward certain academic domains (Wigfield & Eccles, 2002). The assumption is that these judgments are influenced by students' perceptions of capability in these domains, which are the result of interpreting past successes and failures, of social comparison with peers, and feedback from teachers and other adults (Bandura, 1997). This is particularly true in mathematics (Pajares & Graham, 1999), and findings from recent studies suggest that students' pathways into mathematics-related careers begin as early as middle school when students are forming lasting self-perceptions of their academic abilities (Grossman & Porche, 2014; Shoffner et al., 2015). Middle school is also a time when students begin making choices about future coursework in math, science, and technology that will have long-term implications for their academic and career achievements (Eccles, 2009). By high school, these choices become more solidified (Simpkins, Davis-Kean, & Eccles, 2006; Wigfield & Eccles, 2002).

Because of its predictive utility, the self-efficacy construct has received considerable attention within the career development literature. Hackett and Betz's (1981) work that asserts self-efficacy beliefs may be important determinants of educational and career behavior stimulated much of the current research. Mathematics is a critical gateway within the career choice process. Several studies have demonstrated that self-efficacy predicts academic choice behavior (i.e., high school course selection or selection of a college major) and achievements in math and math-related disciplines (Lent & Brown, 2013; Lopez, Lent, Brown, & Gore, 1997). Within the social-cognitive framework, level of mathematics self-efficacy is a critical factor for predicting students' engagement and persistence in the STEM career pipeline (Chemers et al., 2011; Grossman & Porche, 2014).

While many middle school students experience declines in attitudes, including interest and motivation for math, there are significant gender differences regarding confidence and beliefs about competence related to math and that emerge during middle school (Wigfield & Eccles, 2000; Wigfield, Eccles, & Pintrich, 1996). For example, boys and girls tend to report equal levels of confidence in their abilities to do math in elementary school but, by middle school, boys tend to rate themselves as more efficacious than do girls (Betz & Hackett, 1983; Butz & Usher, 2015; Else-Quest, Mineo, & Higgins, 2013; Huang, 2013; Lent, Lopez, & Bieschke, 1991; Pintrich & De Groot, 1990). Several studies have found that middle school boys tend to have higher self-efficacy and outcome expectations for math and science than do girls (Ferry, Fouad, & Smith, 2000; Fouad & Guillen, 2006; Jacobs et al., 2002). Gifted girls are more likely to report under-confidence in mathematics (Pajares, 1996, 2005), and the "confidence gap" that emerges during middle school seems to remain steady over time (Herbert & Stipek, 2005; Jacobs et al., 2002; Marsh, Craven, & Debus, 1998).

The findings from studies on math self-efficacy and gender differences in middle school suggest that promoting positive beliefs about math and math learning and helping to improve students' self-beliefs in math are critical for supporting mathematics-related educational and career decision-making (Chemers et al., 2011; Falk et al., 2017; Grossman & Porche, 2014). Supporting self-efficacy for math is important for most middle school students but may be crucial for girls who often experience significant declines in their feelings of competence in this domain.

Self-Efficacy and Outcome Expectations

Student achievement in math is critical for their future STEM engagement, but many factors are linked inextricably to achievement including attitudes such as interest, self-efficacy, and outcome expectations (Wigfield & Eccles, 2002). If students do not believe they can be successful in a given domain (i.e., have low self-efficacy), they will likely lose interest and fail to persist in the face of challenges (Betz, 2007; Eccles & Wigfield, 2002). If students do not have strong self-efficacy for math, they are less likely to place value on STEM education or be interested in pursuing STEM-related goals and aspirations (Betz, 2007). This is also the case when students have negative outcome expectations for a task. If they believe that pursuing a particular goal will have a negative impact on things such as time or relationships, they tend to place less value on its importance. Similarly, if students have negative outcome expectations related to STEM coursework or careers, they are more likely to avoid both (Sadler, Sonnert, Hazari, & Tai, 2012).

Math Self-Efficacy Intervention

To support student mathematics engagement, achievement, and consideration of future STEM coursework and careers, there is a need for interventions designed to have a positive impact on student self-efficacy, and it is important to focus such efforts in middle school. The preceding sections of this article explained the relationship between self-efficacy and decision-making and made an argument for the need to help strengthen students' self-efficacy, particularly in math, to support their STEM engagement. However, translating theory into practice is not always clear cut. Teachers may not have the time or resources required to develop lesson plans that support student learning beyond the core content areas.

This article presents a carefully designed self-efficacy intervention that educators can integrate into the core academic curriculum. Originally conceived as a school-counselor-led guidance unit, classroom teachers can also deliver this intervention. The author created it with input from the sixth-grade math teachers at the school where it was first implemented and evaluated, but it was (and is) intended to support student self-efficacy and self-regulation behaviors within the context of math learning. It uses mathematics examples, and it is best practice to embed the lessons within the math curriculum as a supplement to math instruction, but it is not intended to teach specific math skills.

As outlined in *This We Believe*, published by the Association for Middle-Level Education (formerly National Middle School Association) (NMSA, 2010), this intervention embodies essential attributes for education. Specifically, it is developmentally responsive and equitable in that it helps to ensure relevant learning opportunities for every student. This intervention is unique in that it supports self-efficacy for a particular group of students—girls—who often experience significant declines in their math self-efficacy in middle school.

As such, it exemplifies the following characteristics: (1) curriculum that is challenging, exploratory, integrative, and relevant, and (2) educators use multiple learning and teaching approaches (NMSA, 2010). The self-efficacy intervention described in this article enacts these characteristics through the provision of skill development that goes beyond academic content and considers important psychological processes that may influence students' abilities and willingness to learn. The pilot intervention took place successfully with sixth grade students, and results from studies examining the outcomes of the intervention demonstrate that students who received the intervention showed significant increases in their self-efficacy and attitudes toward mathematics compared to a waitlist control group (Falco, Crethar, & Bauman, 2008; Falco, Summers, & Bauman, 2010). Notably, in the 2010 study, girls who received the intervention showed a higher rate of growth compared to all other students, including on their self-efficacy for math. These results are compelling and provide evidence that this theoretically based self-efficacy intervention may be particularly beneficial for students at a critical point in their development. The subsequent sections describe the curriculum design principles, theoretical framework, and elements of the intervention. The purpose is to provide the reader with enough detail about the intervention that they could readily implement it in other schools. Complete lesson plans and supplementary materials are available from the author upon request.

Challenging, Exploratory, Integrative, and Relevant Curriculum: Design Principles

Improving students' self-efficacy beliefs, particularly in relation to mathematics learning, is the focus of the intervention described in this article. The curriculum targets students' feelings of self-competence through lessons designed to foster four skills: time management, goal-setting, study habits, and help-seeking. The four skills are behaviors associated with personal agency to activate desired self-efficacy beliefs. Research supports that there is a positive relationship between mechanisms of personal agency and adolescents' self-efficacy (Bandura, 1997; Byrnes, 1998; Pajares, 1996; Pajares & Kranzler, 1995).

The unit consists of two lessons for each skill, beginning with time management, geared specifically toward math learning. For example, time management lessons help students budget their time for studying math and to plan out daily assignments, tests, and quizzes using a weekly schedule. Goal-setting lessons help students set and reach obtainable, personal goals related to their math class. Study-habits lessons help students learn to organize mathematical concepts and learn specific strategies for studying for math. Finally, help-seeking lessons help students become aware of when they do not understand a critical concept and to ask questions that will help elicit the information they need from the teacher in order to understand. The overarching objective of the curriculum is to translate the theoretical concept of self-efficacy into concrete skills related to human agency that students can learn. As students' feelings of self-competence for math increase so, too, should their interest and engagement in math.

Multiple Learning Approaches: Improving Self-Efficacy and Outcome Expectations

Through its focus on self-efficacy, the intervention supports positive outcome expectations in math which are critical for students' academic achievement and STEM interest and engagement (Betz & Hackett, 1983; Dang & Nylund-Gibson, 2017; Falk et al., 2017). Because social-cognitive theory is the theoretical framework that embodies the self-efficacy construct, it provides a method for changing students' perceptions of their own self-efficacy. According to Bandura (1986), five basic cognitive processes influence personal determinants (such as self-efficacy) related to academic motivation: (1) symbolic thought, (2) forethought, (3) vicarious learning, (4) self-regulation, and (5) self-reflection. For example, most people are capable of symbolic thought, which allows them to process the experiences of others, through observation, into mental models that guide their learning and performance. Forethought is the mental representation of future events and can also influence individuals' learning through purposive planning. Vicarious capabilities allow individuals to conceptualize their own success through observing the success of others. Self-regulation occurs when individuals compare their own capabilities regarding a task against a set of standards they maintain for themselves. Self-reflection capabilities refer to individuals' ability to determine what capabilities they have regarding a task through comparison to others (peers) and/or past performance. Accurate self-reflection is essential for the development of self-efficacy (see

Bandura, 1989, for a complete description of these cognitive processes). These five basic capabilities serve as important guidelines for self-efficacy interventions (Schunk, 1996; Zimmerman, 2000; Zimmerman, Bandura, & Martinez-Pons, 1992).

Studies of interventions designed to alter students' self-efficacy beliefs demonstrate the importance of planning, modeling, goal-setting, and learning strategies as effective methods for increasing students' self-regulatory processes, academic motivation, and achievement (Bandura & Schunk, 1981; Bouffard-Bouchard, Parent, & Larivee, 1991; Lent, Brown, & Larking, 1984; Multon, Brown, & Lent, 1991; Schunk, 1989, 1990, 1996; Schunk & Ertmer, 2000). Research also provides evidence of the importance of skill acquisition over verbal persuasion for effectively influencing students' self-efficacy (Bandura & Schunk, 1981; Kramer & Engle, 1981; Wood & Bandura, 1989). The implications from such studies suggest that an intervention designed to increase students' self-efficacy should involve teaching skills related to planning, goal-setting, and learning strategies. See Figure 3.1 for a description of the curriculum design principles.

Lessons also provide students with opportunities for mastery experiences by sequencing cognitive strategies and skills from the relatively simple (time management) to the more complex (help-seeking skills). Beginning with time management, each skill builds on the previous ones so that students can continue to apply what they have already learned to the subsequent skills. Students learn to apply their new skills to their classroom learning and other areas of their lives, and the didactic (processing) component of the intervention provides students with examples of how to do so. Processing questions are generally open-ended and help students reflect on the emotions associated with learning (Gaw, 1979). In other words, through processing, the students learn to assume responsibility for that which they encountered and learned. By utilizing active participation and active processing, the learning event is "more experiential." In a relative educational sense, the learner is more "in-touch" with his or her own learning through bridging or meaning making through the processing (Quinsland & Van Ginkel, 1984). Many of the lessons also support students' math skills such as adding, subtracting, ranking, estimating, creating timelines, and applying logic, for example. See Figure 3.2 for a description of the curriculum scope and sequence.

Intervention Scope and Sequence

Time Management

Middle school is often the first time during students' schooling when they are responsible for assignments in multiple subjects from multiple teachers. Middle school is also a time of increased autonomy for students who

Design Principle	Social-Cognitive Tenet	Description	Learning Experiences
Skill-Based	Agency	Students exercise some control over their thoughts, feelings, and actions	Lessons teach discrete skills: time management, goal- setting, math study skills, and help seeking
Math Specific	Domain Specificity	Students' self- efficacy judgments are domain specific	Lesson activities related to math and math learning
Sequence	Reciprocal Determinism	Learning environment, cognitions, and behavior interact to influence students' self-beliefs; therefore, the environment can be structured to enhance or improve students' self-efficacy	Lesson content sequenced from simple to complex; each lesson builds on prior skills
Process	Self-Reflection	Students evaluate their experiences and thought processes; self-referent thought mediates between knowledge and action	Lesson processing questions provide opportunity for self-reflection and improve accuracy of self-appraisal
Outcomes	Self-Regulation	Students with strong self-efficacy beliefs make better use of meta-cognitive strategies that influence performance	Lessons teach strategies to improve students' self-regulatory practices

Figure 3.1 Middle School Math Self-Efficacy Curriculum Design Principles

must keep track of important dates and assignments with fewer reminders from their teachers (Zimmerman & Cleary, 2006). This might create anxiety for students who have difficulty with personal organization. Research examining the effects of time management skills interventions in middle and high school demonstrates that learning time management skills helps reduce student anxiety. This effect occurs as students gain greater control over their environment (Juvonen & Wentzel, 1996).

Skill *Lesson*	Description/Objective	Cognitive Processes	Self-Efficacy Beliefs
1. Time Management *1) Time Budget* *2) Daily and Weekly Planning*	· Apply time-management and task-management skills · Demonstrate ability to balance school, studies, extracurricular activities, leisure time, and family life · Organize and apply academic information from a variety of sources	· Forethought · · Planning	· ↑ perceived control over environment · ↑ perceived control over environment
2. Goal-Setting *3) Goal-Setting Practice* *4) Smart Goal Evaluation*	· Identify attitudes and behaviors that lead to successful learning · Learn the goal-setting process · Apply knowledge of aptitudes and interests to goal-setting · Identify personal strengths and assets · Establish challenging goals in middle school · Use problem-solving and decision-making skills to assess progress toward educational goals	· Symbolizing · Self-regulation · Self-reflection · Self-reflection	· ↑ Mastery goal-orientation · ↑ Self-regulated learning behaviors
3. Math Study Skills *5) General Study Habits* *6) Common Errors*	· Demonstrate how effort and persistence positively affect learning · Apply knowledge and learning preferences to positively influence school performance · Become a self-directed and independent learner · Accept mistakes as essential to the learning process · Use knowledge of learning styles to positively influence performance	· Self-reflection · Self-regulation	· ↑Self-reflection and accurate self-appraisal · ↑Capability to exercise self-influence · ↑Accurate self-appraisal and causal attribution
4. Help-Seeking *7) Getting Help* *8) Asking Questions*	· Use communication skills to know when and how to ask for help when needed · Seek information and support from faculty, staff, family, and peers · Learn and apply critical thinking skills · Become a self-directed learner	· Self-reflection · Self-regulation	· ↑Self-reflection and metacognition · ↑Situational adaptivity · ↑Feelings of autonomy

Figure 3.2 Middle School Math Self-Efficacy Curriculum Scope and Sequence

Lesson one: "time budget": Time management involves the cognitive processes of forethought and planning. To teach time management skills, the first lesson in the "Skill-Builders" unit introduces the concept of planning through an activity called "Creating a Time Budget." Students generate a to-do list including their daily activities and the amount of time it takes to complete each one. They must divide their activities into two categories: things they "have to" do, such as homework and chores, and things they "want to" do, such as play on the computer and watch TV. Then, they complete a "time budget" where they include each of their daily activities and make it add up to 24 hours. Students may realize that they must shorten or eliminate some activities if there is not enough time to do them all. The teacher asks processing questions such as, "How did you decide what activities get shortened?" or, "Did anyone have extra time left on his or her budget?" The teacher facilitates a discussion on the challenge of creating enough time to complete all the activities one must do and wants to do in a day. The teacher can also explain that, when students learn to manage time, they might be surprised at how much they can accomplish. The teacher can also model time management by showing students an example of a completed "time budget" or by providing students with other real-life examples of schedules (such as the school day).

The lesson objective is to increase students' perceived control over their environment through budgeting time. Additionally, students will estimate the amount of time needed for each activity and adding or subtracting time from the "time budget" to make it sum to 24 hours.

Lesson two: "daily and weekly planning": The second time management lesson teaches students strategies for daily and weekly planning. Once students have balanced their "time budgets," the next step is to teach them how to plan and organize their time into a weekly schedule. The lesson begins with a self-reflection activity. Students complete a worksheet that requires them to describe what they are doing at different times of the day during different days of the week. They will think specifically about math class and what they will be doing each day of the week during that week. The second part of the lesson is for students to complete a weekly plan for math class. They fill in the topic, class work, homework, and any tests or quizzes they might have for each day of the week. The teacher might encourage them to use different colors for important dates to help them remember, and to check off assignments they have completed and turned in as a way to prevent missing work. The teacher asks processing questions such as "Did you find this challenging?" and "How do you feel now that you've tried it?" Class discussion should help students understand the connection between thought and action through planning. The teacher helps students reflect on the affective (emotional) experience of learning to control time. The lesson objective is to reinforce students' perceived control over time and their ability to apply time management skills to planning their weekly math assignments. Another objective is to increase students' awareness of time and planned activities. As time and planning become more conscious, students can apply their skills to weekly planning. Students will rank activities (prioritize) according to time, urgency, consequences, or the importance of each activity. They will also make a timeline and extend their plan beyond one day.

Goal-Setting

Goal-setting involves the cognitive processes of symbolizing, forethought, self-reflection, and self-regulation. Students must first conceive of a goal that they would like to strive for (symbolize), articulate the steps necessary to reach the goal (forethought), assess their progress along the way (self-reflection), and adjust their plan if necessary (self-regulation). Goal-setting plays an important role in students' self-regulation and academic performance (Zimmerman et al., 1992). Academic self-regulation refers to the degree to which students use metacognitive, motivational, and proactive processes to direct their learning (Zimmerman, 1986, 1990). From a social-cognitive view, self-regulated learners employ these strategies by setting challenging but appropriate goals for themselves. Research indicates that self-regulated learners have high self-efficacy for their capabilities (Zimmerman, 2000), and several studies have demonstrated that teaching low-achieving students to set proximal goals for themselves increases their self-efficacy, their academic achievement, and their interest in the subject matter (Eccles, 1983; Garcia & Pintrich, 1994; Schunk, 1989).

Lesson three: goal-setting practice: To teach goal-setting skills, the third lesson in the unit introduces the concept through use of a stair-case analogy. The teacher begins the lesson by asking students, "What is a goal?" After listening to the student responses, the teacher clarifies that a goal is a desired accomplishment that a person strives for. The teacher asks students, "What is an objective?" and clarifies that objectives are small steps taken to reach a goal. Then, the teacher can use the staircase analogy to describe the process of setting and achieving goals. The top of the staircase represents the goal. It clearly defines for what to strive. The steps represent objectives; taking small steps instead of one giant leap helps a person get to the goal without getting too tired or losing balance. As one climbs each step (or accomplish each objective), one moves closer to the goal. Each step (objective) provides feedback on how well one is doing; the number of steps climbed successfully helps to measure progress. Climbing all the steps represents reaching the goal. The teacher facilitates class discussion about the work it takes to achieve goals, distributes copies of the Goal Setting Practice Worksheet, and instructs students to use the worksheet to help them plan out the necessary steps for achieving their goal.

The lesson objective is to increase students' mastery-orientation toward problem-solving and proactive, self-regulated learning behaviors. The staircase analogy helps students focus on achieved progress and provides them with a way to utilize feedback. The lesson should also increase students' perceptions of their ability to control desired outcomes. Students will also use logic because goal-setting involves strategy—breaking up the end goal into smaller objectives that progress in a logical order.

Lesson four: SMART goal evaluation: The fourth lesson in the unit teaches students how to evaluate their goals using the SMART method. SMART is an acronym that stands for Specific, Measurable, Attainable, Rewarding, and Timely. It is used widely in various contexts involving personal goal-setting (Loo, 2006; Meyer, 2002). The purpose of the SMART approach is to help students create goals that are effective and achievable. The teacher begins the lesson by asking students to think about the goals they wrote for themselves during the previous lesson and explains that this lesson is to help them learn how to evaluate their goals so that they are more likely to accomplish them.

Next, the teacher introduces the SMART acronym and explains what each letter stands for. Then, the teacher facilitates class discussion about each of the SMART guidelines. For example, the teacher can begin by asking students what "specific" means to them. The teacher gives students strategies for generating specific goals, such as writing them down. The teacher asks students to give examples and uses class discussion to point out goals that are specific. The teacher also asks processing questions such as: "Why do you think specific goals work better than general goals?" Then, the teacher proceeds through the remaining letters in the acronym in a similar way until students are familiar with the process of evaluating goals using this approach. After this, the teacher hands out the SMART Evaluation Worksheet (see Figure 3.3) and instructs students to re-examine their goals from last time and evaluate them using the rubric on the worksheet.

The teacher ends the lesson with a class discussion about the SMART approach. Some processing questions might include, "Did your goals change after using the SMART approach?" and "How can you use the SMART approach in this class?"

The objective of the lesson is to reinforce a mastery-orientation toward problem-solving and to provide students with a concrete way to generate feedback for themselves so that they can increase self-reflection and their

	Not at all ← ⟶ Completely									
	1	2	3	4	5	6	7	8	9	10
S-pecific										
M-easurable										
A-ttainable										
R-ewarding										
T-imely										

Figure 3.3 SMART Goal Evaluation Worksheet

ability to self-evaluate. The lesson should also reinforce students' ability to control desired outcomes through planning. Students will also use their measurement skills by learning how to quantify their objectives and goals so that they know when they have accomplished them. Students should also use their estimation skills to create a realistic timeline for accomplishing their goals.

Math Study Skills

Arguably, study skills involve each of the five cognitive capabilities outlined in the social-cognitive theory of academic motivation, but they mainly involve self-reflection and self-regulation. Students must be aware of their own preferences and habits (self-reflection) to develop more adaptive strategies for studying and learning (self-regulation). The word "skill" itself, versus "intelligence" or "talent", implies that good study skills are not necessarily innate; students acquire and improve study skills through training and practice, which is important to note because of the implications for improving self-directed learning. Effective study skills interventions teach skills in context, involve tasks in domain-specific content, and promote metacognitive awareness (Hattie, Biggs, & Purdie, 1996). Furthermore, a report from the National Center for Education Research (National Center for Education Research (NCER), 2007) on effective strategies for encouraging students in math and science recommends teaching study skills to demonstrate that cognitive abilities can be improved and expanded. Students who believe that their cognitive capabilities are fixed are more likely to experience decreased confidence and performance (Dweck, 2007).

Lesson five: general study habits: The fifth lesson in the "Skill-Builders" unit teaches general study habits in math and helps students understand and believe that they can acquire better study skills. The lesson begins with self-reflection to help students examine their current study habits. The teacher asks the class to describe how they usually feel when it is time to sit down and study math and makes note of their responses. The teacher explains that studying math is done often by doing problems. Also, each concept in math builds on concepts that are already learned. Good study habits help students become more efficient, so practice is important. The teacher explains to students that they will become faster and be able to remember more if they make good math study habits a part of their lives.

Next, the teacher asks the class to take a few minutes to review their current study habits by completing the Study Habits Checklist Worksheet. After students complete the worksheet, the teacher asks some processing questions such as, "How many of you learned something about yourselves?" and "What are some of the things you do that keep you from having good study habits in math?" The teacher uses the class discussion to segue into a discussion on strategies for studying math and strategies for math test-taking. The teacher explains to the class that, in many ways, good study habits in math involve skills that they have learned so far—time management and goal-setting play a big role in learning to study better. The teacher then discusses each strategy with the class and asks students to try and pick at least one that they can make a part of their daily routine. Afterward, the teacher asks the class to recall each of the strategies. The lesson objective is to improve students' self-reflection and self-appraisal capabilities. The lesson reinforces students' capability to exercise self-influence through purposive behavior (planning and managing study habits). Students use skills such as division and ranking by learning to break tasks into manageable chunks either by time (length of time needed), difficulty (easiest to hardest), or quantity (number of problems).

Lesson six: common errors: The sixth lesson in the unit teaches students how to identify common mistakes when doing math. The lesson uses an exploration exercise to help students identify common errors they make and class discussion provides students with specific strategies for correcting them. The teacher begins by asking students to get a copy of a recently completed exam, quiz, or homework assignment. Preferably, students will have more than one type of assignment to use for the activity, and it is a good idea to let students know ahead of time so that they can come prepared. The teacher asks students if they have ever noticed that there are different types of math problems and asks them to list the different types. Then, the teacher explains that studying for math may take more time than other subjects because math requires time to solve problems. The teacher reminds students to use their time management skills to give themselves enough time to do all their math homework—if they skip parts or rush through it, they will not learn important concepts as well as they should. The teacher should explain that math builds on everything learned before, so it is important for students to learn each concept completely as they go. The teacher then asks students to reflect on their beliefs about math learning. Processing questions might include, "Do you believe that a person has to be naturally smart to learn math?" and "Do you believe that anyone can learn math?" Explain that the latter is true and that they can be actively involved in managing their learning process in math.

To begin the exploration exercise, the teacher distributes a copy of the Common Errors Checklist Worksheet to each of the students. The teacher explains to the class that students usually make mistakes in math learning due to a few common errors. It is important that students learn to identify these common errors so that they can correct them and manage their math learning. The teacher instructs students to use the worksheet to help them analyze their tests, quizzes, and/or homework to identify their most common errors. To do this, students must look at each problem they got wrong, identify the type of error they made, and see if there is a pattern. For each of the six types of common errors on the worksheet, there is a strategy for correcting it. After students complete the exploration exercise, the teacher facilitates a discussion about correcting each type of error and provides additional strategies for improved math study skills (all information is contained in the worksheet). Additional processing questions might include, "What did you learn about yourself after doing this exercise?" and "How can you use these strategies to manage your math learning?"

The objective of the lesson is to increase students' self-reflection and self-regulation by helping them become more aware of their mistakes and by providing them with strategies for correcting them. The lesson should also increase the accuracy of their self-evaluations and causal attributions. Students learn to identify and correct mistakes, and they discover that mistakes are not necessarily caused by personal deficiency or low ability. In this exercise, students are learning to evaluate and monitor their task performance through careful examination of the process of problem-solving.

Help-Seeking Skills

Help-seeking in academic settings refers to students' abilities and/or willingness to ask peers, parents, teachers, or others for help when they are having difficulty understanding material and have exhausted other strategies for learning. The cognitive processes involved in help-seeking are self-reflection (recognizing the need for help) and self-regulation (asking for help when needed and using strategies to elicit high-level help). Research demonstrates that help-seeking behavior is highly adaptive because it promotes mastery-goal-oriented achievement behavior (Karabenick & Newman, 2013). Students with a mastery-goal-orientation are more likely to seek instrumental, autonomous help when needed whereas students with a performance-goal-orientation are more likely to avoid seeking help or to seek expedient help when they do (Arbreton, 1993, 1998; Butler & Neuman, 1995; Karabenik, 2003, 2004; Ryan & Pintrich, 1997). Help-seeking is a concept within the framework of self-regulation and achievement motivation. An important study examining student help-seeking behavior in mathematics demonstrated that students who asked specific questions about how to solve math problems received higher level help, more frequently applied the help they received on their own, and obtained higher levels of achievement than students who only asked general-level questions or who gave expressions of confusion (Webb, Ing, Kersting, & Nemer, 2006). Students typically avoid seeking help when they need it because of perceived threats to their self-worth (Karabenick & Newman, 2013). The help-seeking lessons in this unit help students overcome these fears by providing concrete strategies for getting help and asking questions along with opportunities to practice their skills in a cooperative learning environment.

Lesson seven: getting help: The seventh lesson in the unit introduces the concept of getting help. The lesson begins with a self-reflection activity to help students examine their beliefs about getting help, and class discussion helps students increase their self-reflection capabilities and helps them overcome perceived threats to self-worth when asking for help. The teacher distributes a copy of the Getting Help Worksheet to each student and allows them about three to five minutes to complete it. After students finish the worksheet, the teacher facilitates a discussion focusing on a few key questions such as, "Do you feel comfortable asking questions during class?" and "Can you think of a time when you have wanted to ask a question in class but didn't?" and "What prevented you from asking a question when you needed to?" The teacher helps students process their responses. Common themes are likely to be: not wanting to seem stupid, embarrassment, not knowing when to ask, and not knowing what to ask. The teacher explains to the class that these feelings are very common and that almost everyone has been afraid to ask a question at some point during their life.

Next, the teacher explains to the class that, not only will asking questions help them learn the material, it will help them accomplish their goals and feel good about themselves because they will gain insight, understanding, and skills that they can use in all areas of their lives. The teacher can continue to help students process their feelings regarding getting help, guiding them toward accepting the need for help as a positive instead of a negative. When a student shares his or her feelings, the teacher asks the class to give feedback. The lesson ends by reviewing the five tips for getting help (information on the worksheet), processing each tip together, and asking students to recall the tips at the end. The teacher can also share the Help-Seeking Affirmations to model help-seeking behavior.

The lesson objective is to increase students' sense of autonomy and confidence by teaching instrumental help-seeking strategies. The self-reflection exercise and class discussion should help students recognize the need to get help and to overcome their fears for getting help when they need it. Students will not use explicit math skills, but they will learn to identify skills, techniques, and strategies that apply to problem-solving and they will learn to recognize the need to ask for assistance during problem-solving.

Lesson eight: asking questions: The final lesson in the unit gives students an opportunity to practice the help-seeking strategies that they learned in the previous lesson. See Appendix for sample lesson plans and materials for help-seeking.

The teacher begins the lesson by asking students if they have any questions from last time and allow for a few minutes of class discussion about getting help and the feelings students experience when asking questions. The teacher begins the group activity by explaining to students that one of the best ways to learn how and when to ask the right questions is to practice. The teacher places students into groups of four or five and gives each group a copy of the *Getting Help Practice Worksheet* and a "problem scenario" (see Appendix) which should be written on a piece of paper or index card beforehand. Explain to the groups that they should work together to answer the questions on the worksheet and allow 10–12 minutes for them to complete the activity.

When groups finish, the teacher asks each group to share its "problem scenario" and the questions they generated to help solve the problem. The teacher facilitates discussion by giving each group specific feedback about the questions they generated, emphasizing the importance of instrumental help-seeking behaviors (Karabenick & Newman, 2013) such as, "I don't understand why you did . . ." and "Can you show me how to do . . ." The teacher ends the lesson with a class discussion on the importance of getting help when needed. The teacher validates help-seeking behaviors as an important strategy for managing the learning process, and re-reads the Help-Seeking Affirmations.

To help students fully process the lessons in the unit, it is best for the teacher to meet with the class after completing all eight lessons to review the material and ask students to share their experiences using their new skills. A short quiz that helps students recall information from each of the lessons part of the unit is provided in the lesson plan. The teacher can encourage students to use their skills in each of their classes and to refer to their packets as a tool for studying in other subject areas.

Summary

A carefully designed intervention, such as the one described in this article, appears to have strong potential for preventing the decline in feelings of competence—particularly in math—that emerge during early adolescence. A number of factors may ultimately influence students' engagement in mathematics and math-related disciplines, but the relationship between self-efficacy and choice is fairly well established (Eccles, Wigfield, Harold, & Blumenfeld, 1993; Jacobs et al., 2002; Meece, Wigfield, & Eccles, 1990). Therefore, an intervention that can improve participating students', especially girls', self-efficacy for math may be particularly valuable in terms of influencing their future engagement in STEM careers. It would be worthwhile for future research to examine the longer term impacts of such interventions.

This self-efficacy intervention is one way that teachers can utilize multiple learning approaches to empower students with a heightened sense of agency and control over their own learning. For students in middle school who may be experiencing more negative attitudes toward math and/or declines in their perceptions of self-competence in this domain, a self-efficacy intervention has the potential to impact these beliefs in a positive way by guiding students away from the idea that math ability is innate or fixed and focusing on math learning as a skill that can be mastered through practice. The intervention emphasizes dimensions of learning beyond the academic content and, as such, activates important psychological processes that can support student achievement and engagement in ways that more traditional approaches might not.

References

American Association of University Women. (2010). *Why so few? Women in science, technology, engineering, and mathematics.* Washington, DC: Author.

Arbreton, A. (1993). *When getting help is helpful: Developmental, cognitive, and motivational influences on students' academic help-seeking.* Ann Arbor, MI: University of Michigan.

Arbreton, A. (Ed.). (1998). *Student goal orientation and help-seeking strategy use.* Mahwah, NJ: Lawrence Erlbaum Associates.

Bandura, A. (1977). Self-efficacy: Toward a unifying theory of behavioral change. *Psychological Review, 84,* 191–215.

Bandura, A. (1986). The explanatory and predictive scope of self-efficacy theory. *Journal of Social and Clinical Psychology, 4,* 359–373. https://doi.org/10.1521/jscp.1986.4.3.359

Bandura, A. (1989). Regulation of cognitive processes through perceived self-efficacy. *Developmental Psychology, 25,* 729–735. https://doi.org/10.1037/0012-1649.25.5.729

Bandura, A. (1997). *Self-efficacy: The exercise of control.* New York: Freeman.

Bandura, A., & Schunk, D. H. (1981). Cultivating competence, self-efficacy, and intrinsic interest through proximal self-motivation. *Journal of Personality and Social Psychology, 41*(3), 586. https://doi.org/10.1037/0022-3514.41.3.586

Betz, N. E. (2007). Career self-efficacy: Exemplary recent research and emerging directions. *Journal of Career Assessment, 15*(4), 403–422. https://doi.org/10.1177/1069072707305759

Betz, N. E., & Hackett, G. (1983). The relationship of mathematics self-efficacy expectations to the selection of science-based college majors. *Journal of Vocational Behavior, 23*(3), 329–345. https://doi.org/10.1016/0001-8791(83)90046-5

Bouffard-Bouchard, T., Parent, S., & Larivee, S. (1991). Influence of self-efficacy on self-regulation and performance among junior and senior high-school age students. *International Journal of Behavioral Development, 14,* 153–164. https://doi.org/10.1177/016502549101400203

Butler, R., & Neuman, O. (1995). Effects of task and ego achievement goals on help-seeking behaviors and attitudes. *Journal of Educational Psychology, 87,* 261–271. https://doi.org/10.1037/0022-0663.87.2.261

Butz, A. R., & Usher, E. L. (2015). Salient sources of early adolescents' self-efficacy in two domains. *Contemporary Educational Psychology, 42,* 49–61. https://doi.org/10.1016/j.cedpsych.2015.04.001

Byrnes, J. B. (1998). *The nature and development of self-regulated decision making*. Hillsdale, NJ: Lawrence Erlbaum Associates.

Chemers, M. M., Zurbriggen, E. L., Syed, M., Goza, B. K., & Bearman, S. (2011). The role of efficacy and identity in science career commitment among underrepresented minority students. *Journal of Social Issues, 67*, 469–491. https://doi.org/10.1111/josi.2011.67.issue-3

Dang, M., & Nylund-Gibson, K. (2017). Connecting math attitudes with STEM career, attainment: A latent class analysis approach. *Teachers College Record, 119*(6), 1–38.

Dweck, C. S. (2007). *Is math a gift? Beliefs that put females at risk* (pp. 47–55). Washington, DC: American Psychological Association.

Eccles, J. S. (1983). Expectancies, values, and academic behaviors. In J. T. Spence (Ed.), *Achievement and achievement motives* (pp. 75–146). San Francisco, CA: Freeman.

Eccles, J. S. (2009). Who am I and what am I going to do with my life? Personal and collective identities as motivators of action. *Educational Psychologist, 44*, 78–89. https://doi.org/10.1080/00461520902832368

Eccles, J. S., & Wigfield, A. (2002). Motivational beliefs, values, and goals. *Annual Review of Psychology, 53*, 109–132. https://doi.org/10.1146/annurev.psych.53.100901.135153

Eccles, J. S., Wigfield, A., Harold, R. D., & Blumenfeld, P. (1993). Age and gender differences in children's self- and task perceptions during elementary school. *Child Development, 64*, 830–847.

Else-Quest, N. M., Mineo, C. C., & Higgins, A. (2013). Math and science attitudes and achievement at the intersection of gender and ethnicity. *Psychology of Women Quarterly, 37*(3), 293–309. https://doi.org/10.1177/0361684313480694

Falco, L. D., Crethar, H., & Bauman, S. (2008). Skill-builders: Improving middle school students' self-beliefs for learning mathematics. *Professional School Counseling, 11*(4), 229–235. https://doi.org/10.5330/PSC. n.2010-11.229

Falco, L. D., Summers, J. J., & Bauman, S. (2010). Encouraging mathematics participation through improved self-efficacy: A school counseling outcomes study. *Educational Research and Evaluation, 16*(6), 529–549. https://doi.org/10.108 0/13803611.2011.555101

Falk, N. A., Rottinghaus, P. J., Casanova, T. N., Borgen, F. H., & Betz, N. E. (2017). Expanding women's participation in STEM: Insights from parallel measures of self-efficacy and interests. *Journal of Career Assessment, 25*, 571–584. https://doi.org/10.1177/1069072716665822

Ferry, T. R., Fouad, N. A., & Smith, P. L. (2000). The role of family context in a social cognitive model for career-related choice behavior: A math and science perspective. *Journal of Vocational Behavior, 57*, 348–364. https://doi.org/10.1006/jvbe.1999.1743

Fouad, N. A., & Guillen, A. (2006). Outcome expectations: Looking to the past and potential future. *Journal of Career Assessment, 14*, 130–142. https://doi.org/10.1177/1069072705281370

Franklin, D. (2013). A practical guide to gender diversity for computer science faculty. *Synthesis Lectures on Professionalism and Career Advancement for Scientists and Engineers, 1*, 1–81. https://doi.org/10.2200/S00495ED1V01Y201304PRO002

Garcia, T., & Pintrich, P. R. (1994). Regulating motivation and cognition in the classroom: The role of self-schemas and self-regulatory strategies. In D. Schunk &

B. Zimmerman (Eds.), *Self-regulation of learning and performance: Issues and educational applications* (pp. 127–154). Hillsdale, NJ: Erlbaum.

Gaw, B. A. (1979). Processing questions: An aid to completing the learning cycle. In J. E. Jones & J. W. Pfeiffer (Eds.), *The 1979 annual handbook for group facilitators* (pp. 147–153). San Diego, CA: University Associates.

Grossman, J. M., & Porche, M. V. (2014). Perceived gender and racial/ethnic barriers to STEM success. *Urban Education, 49*, 698–727. https://doi.org/10.1177/0042085913481364

Hackett, G., & Betz, N. E. (1981). A self-efficacy approach to the career development of women. *Journal of Vocational Behavior, 18*, 326–339. https://doi.org/10.1016/0001-8791(81)90019-1

Hattie, J., Biggs, J., & Purdie, N. (1996). Effects of learning skills interventions on student learning: A meta-analysis. *Review of Educational Research, 66*, 99–136. https://doi.org/10.3102/00346543066002099

Herbert, J., & Stipek, D. (2005). The emergence of gender differences in children's perceptions of their academic competence. *Journal of Applied Developmental Psychology, 26*, 276–295. https://doi.org/10.1016/j. appdev.2005.02.007

Huang, C. (2013). Gender differences in academic self-efficacy: A meta-analysis. *European Journal of Psychology of Education, 28*(1), 1–35. https://doi.org/10.1007/s10212-011-0097-y

Jacobs, J. E., Lanza, S., Osgood, D. W., Eccles, J. S., & Wigfield, A. (2002). Changes in children's self-competence and values: Gender and domain differences across grades one through twelve. *Child Development, 73*(2), 509–527.

Juvonen, J., & Wentzel, K. R. (Eds.). (1996). *Social motivation: Understanding children's school adjustment.* New York: Cambridge University Press.

Karabenik, S. A. (2003). Help-seeking in large college classes: A person-centered approach. *Contemporary Educational Psychology, 28*, 37–58. https://doi.org/10.1016/S0361-476X(02)00012-7

Karabenik, S. A. (2004). Perceived achievement goal structure and college student help seeking. *Journal of Educational Psychology, 96*(3), 569–581. https://doi.org/10.1037/0022-0663.96.3.569

Karabenick, S. A., & Newman, R. S. (Eds.). (2013). *Help seeking in academic settings: Goals, groups, and contexts.* London: Routledge.

Kramer, J. J., & Engle, R. W. (1981). Teaching awareness of strategic behavior in combination with strategy training: Effects on children's memory performance. *Journal of Experimental Child Psychology, 32*, 513–530.

Lent, R. W., & Brown, S. D. (2013). Social cognitive model of career self-management: Toward a unifying view of adaptive career behavior across the life span. *Journal of Counseling Psychology, 60*, 557. https://doi.org/10.1037/a0033446

Lent, R. W., Brown, S. D., & Larking, K. C. (1984). Relation of self-efficacy expectations to academic achievement and persistence. *Journal of Counseling Psychology, 31*, 356–362. https://doi.org/10.1037/0022-0167.31.3.356

Lent, R. W., Lopez, F. G., & Bieschke, K. J. (1991). Mathematics self-efficacy: Sources and relation to science-based career choice. *Journal of Counseling Psychology, 38*, 424. https://doi.org/10.1037/0022-0167.38.4.424

Loo, T. (2006). *SMART goal setting 101: The definitive guide to goal achievement* [Electronic version]. Retrieved from www.synergyinstituteonline.com

Lopez, F. G., Lent, R. W., Brown, S. D., & Gore, P. A. (1997). Role of social—cognitive expectations in high school students' mathematics-related interest and performance. *Journal of Counseling Psychology, 44*, 44. https://doi.org/10.1037/0022-0167.44.1.44

Marsh, H. W., Craven, R., & Debus, R. (1998). Structure, stability, and development of young children's self-concepts: A multicohort—multioccasion study. *Child Development, 69*, 1030–1053.

Meece, J. L., Wigfield, A., & Eccles, J. S. (1990). Predictors of math anxiety and its consequences for young adolescents' course enrollment intentions and performances in mathematics. *Journal of Educational Psychology, 82*, 60–70. https://doi.org/10.1037/0022-0663.82.1.60

Meyer, P. J. (2002). *24 keys that bring complete success.* Alachua, FL: Bridge-Logos.

Midgley, C., Feldlaufer, H., & Eccles, J. S. (1989). Change in teacher efficacy and student self-and task-related beliefs in mathematics during the transition to junior high school. *Journal of Educational Psychology, 81*(2), 247. https://doi.org/10.1037/0022-0663.81.2.247

Multon, K. D., Brown, S. D., & Lent, R. W. (1991). Relation of self-efficacy beliefs to academic outcomes: A meta-analytic investigation. *Journal of Counseling Psychology, 38*(1), 30. https://doi.org/10.1037/0022-0167.38.1.30

National Academy of Science (NAS). (2007). Rising above the gathering storm: Energizing and employing America for a brighter economic future. *Committee on Prospering in the Global Economy of the 21st Century.* Retrieved from www.nap.edu/catalog11463.html

National Center for Education Research (NCER). (2007). *Encouraging girls in math and science: IES practice guide.* Washington, DC: National Center for Education Research.

National Center for Education Statistics (NCES). (2012). *STEM in postsecondary education: Entrance, attrition, and coursetaking among 2003–04 beginning postsecondary students.* Retrieved from www.nces.ed.gov/pubs2013/2013152.pdf

National Center for Education Statistics (NCES). (2016). Status and trends in the education of racial and ethnic groups. *Indicator 24: STEM degrees.* Retrieved from https://nces.ed.gov/programs/raceindicators/indicator_reg.asp

National Middle School Association. (2010). *This we believe: Keys to educating young adolescents.* Westerville, OH: Author.

National Science Foundation. (2015). *Women, minorities, and persons with disabilities in science and engineering: 2015* (Special Report NSF 11–309). Arlington, VA: Author. Retrieved from www.nsf. gov/2015/nsf15311/tables/cfm

Pajares, F. (1996). Self-efficacy beliefs and mathematical problem-solving of gifted students. *Contemporary Educational Psychology, 21*, 325–344.

Pajares, F. (2005). Gender differences in mathematics self-efficacy beliefs. In A. M. Gallagher & J. C. Kaufman (Eds.), *Gender differences in mathematics: An integrative psychological approach* (pp. 294–315). Boston, MA: Cambridge University Press.

Pajares, F., & Graham, L. (1999). Self-efficacy, motivation constructs, and mathematics performance of entering middle school students. *Contemporary Educational Psychology, 24*(2), 124–139. https://doi.org/10.1006/ceps.1998.0991

Pajares, F., & Kranzler, J. (1995). Self-efficacy beliefs and general mental ability in mathematical problem-solving. *Contemporary Educational Psychology, 20*(4), 426–443. https://doi.org/10.1006/ceps.1995.1029

Pintrich, P. R., & De Groot, E. (1990, April). *Quantitative and qualitative perspectives on student motivational beliefs and self-regulated learning.* Paper presented at the Annual Meeting of the American Educational Research Association, Boston, MA. doi:10.1099/00221287-136-2-327

Quinsland, L. K., & Van Ginkel, A. (1984). How to process experience. *Journal of Experiential Education*, 7, 8–13. https://doi.org/10.1177/105382598400700202

Ryan, A. M., & Pintrich, P. R. (1997). "Should I ask for help?" The role of motivation and attitudes in adolescents' help seeking in math class. *Journal of Educational Psychology*, 89, 329–341. https://doi.org/10.1037/0022-0663.89.2.329

Sadler, P. M., Sonnert, G., Hazari, Z., & Tai, R. (2012). Stability and volatility of STEM career interest in high school: A gender study. *Science Education*, 96, 411–427. https://doi.org/10.1002/sce.21007

Schunk, D. H. (1989). Social cognitive theory and self-regulated learning. In B. J. Zimmerman & D. H Schunk (Eds.), *Self-regulated learning and academic achievement: Theory, research, and practice* (pp. 83–110). New York: Springer Verlag.

Schunk, D. H. (1990). Goal setting and self-efficacy during self-regulated learning. *Educational Psychologist*, 25(1), 71–86. https://doi.org/10.1207/s15326985 ep2501_6

Schunk, D. H. (1996). *Learning theories: An educational perspective*. Englewood Cliffs, NJ: Prentice Hall Inc.

Schunk, D. H., & Ertmer, P. A. (2000). Self-regulation and academic learning: Self-efficacy enhancing interventions. In M. Boekaerts, P. R. Pintrich, & M. Zeidner (Eds.), *Handbook of self-regulation* (pp. 631–649). Cambridge, MA: Academic Press.

Shoffner, M. F., Newsome, D., Barrio Minton, C. A., & Wachter-Morris, C. A. (2015). A qualitative exploration of the STEM career-related outcome expectations of young adolescents. *Journal of Career Development*, 42, 102–116. https://doi.org/10.1177/0894845314544033

Simpkins, S. D., Davis-Kean, P. E., & Eccles, J. S. (2006). Math and science motivation: A longitudinal examination of the links between choices and beliefs. *Developmental Psychology*, 42, 70–83. https://doi.org/10.1037/0012-1649.42.1.70

Skaalvik, E. M., Federici, R. A., & Klassen, R. M. (2015). Mathematics achievement and self-efficacy: Relations with motivation for mathematics. *International Journal of Educational Research*, 72, 129–136. https://doi.org/10.1016/j.ijer.2015.06.008

Tai, R. H., Liu, C. Q., Maltese, A. V., & Fan, X. (2006). Planning early for careers in science. *Life Science*, 312, 1143–1144.

Webb, N. M., Ing, M., Kersting, N., & Nemer, K. M. (2006). Help seeking in cooperative learning groups. In S. A. K. R. S. Newman (Ed.), *Help seeking in academic contexts* (pp. 45–115). Mahwah, NJ: Lawrence Erlbaum Associates.

Wigfield, A., & Eccles, J. S. (2000). Expectancy—Value theory of achievement motivation. *Contemporary Educational Psychology*, 25(1), 68–81. https://doi.org/10.1006/ceps.1999.1015

Wigfield, A., & Eccles, J. S. (Eds.). (2002). *Development of achievement motivation*. New York: Elsevier.

Wigfield, A., Eccles, J. S., & Pintrich, P. R. (1996). Development between the ages of 11 and 25. In D. C. Berliner & R. C. Calfee (Eds.), *Handbook of educational psychology* (pp. 148–185). New York: Lawrence Erlbaum & Associates, Inc.

Wood, R., & Bandura, A. (1989). Impact of conceptions of ability on self-regulatory mechanisms and complex decision making. *Journal of Personality and Social Psychology*, 56, 407. https://doi.org/10.1037/0022-3514.56.3.407

Zimmerman, B. J. (1986). Becoming a self-regulated learner: Which are the key subprocesses? *Contemporary Educational Psychology, 11*(4), 307–313. https://doi.org/10.1016/0361-476X(86)90027-5

Zimmerman, B. J. (1990). Self-regulated learning and academic achievement: An overview. *Educational Psychologist, 25*(1), 3–17. https://doi.org/10.1207/s15326985ep2501_2

Zimmerman, B. J. (2000). Self-efficacy: An essential motive to learn. *Contemporary Educational Psychology, 25*, 82–91. https://doi.org/10.1006/ceps.1999.1016

Zimmerman, B. J., Bandura, A., & Martinez-Pons, M. (1992). Self-motivation for academic attainment: The role of self-efficacy beliefs and personal goal setting. *American Educational Research Journal, 29*, 663–676. https://doi.org/10.3102/00028312029003663

Zimmerman, B. J., & Cleary, T. J. (2006). Adolescents' development of personal agency: The role of self-efficacy beliefs and self-regulatory skill. In T. Urdan & F. Pajares (Eds.), *Self-efficacy beliefs of adolescents* (pp. 45–69). Greenwich, CT: Information Age.

Appendix

Grade 6—Activity 7

Introduction to Getting Help

Activity: Getting Help Worksheet. Lesson begins with a self-reflection activity (questionnaire) to help students examine their beliefs about getting help. Counselor facilitates discussion about knowing when you need help and how to get it.

>   **Implementation time:** 30 minutes
>   **Materials:** Getting Help Worksheet

Objectives

Self-Efficacy Beliefs: Increase students' self-reflection capabilities. Class discussion should help them overcome perceived threats to self-worth when asking for help. Increase students' sense of autonomy by learning instrumental help-seeking strategies.

Other Skills: Identifying skills, techniques, and strategies that can be elicit help when needed. Recognizing when to ask for assistance during problem-solving.

Assessment

Successful completion of the Getting Help Worksheet, and teacher/counselor should ask students to recall each of the Tips for Getting Help When You Need It.

ASCA College- and Career Readiness Standard(s)

M 2.	Self-confidence in ability to succeed.
B-LS 4.	Apply self-motivation and self-direction to learning
B-SMS 7.	Demonstrate effective coping skills when faced with a problem

B-SS 8. Demonstrate advocacy skills and ability to assert self, when necessary

Grade 6—Activity 7

Lesson Plan: Getting Help

1. Begin lesson with a self-reflection activity to explore students' beliefs regarding help-seeking.
2. Provide each student with a Getting Help Worksheet and allow 3–5 minutes for them to complete it.
3. After students finish the worksheet, teacher/counselor should facilitate a class discussion focusing on a few key questions:

   - How many of you feel comfortable asking questions during class?
   - How many of you can think of a time when you have wanted to ask a question in class but didn't?
   - What prevented you from asking a question when you needed to?

4. Teacher/counselor should help students process their responses. Common themes are likely to be:

   - I don't want to seem stupid.
   - I am embarrassed.
   - I can't seem to find the right time to ask.
   - I don't know how to ask the right question.

5. Explain to the class that these feelings are very common and that almost everyone has been afraid to ask a question at some point during their life. The important thing to remember is that knowing when and how to ask questions might be the most important thing you'll ever learn in school. Not only will it help you learn, getting help by asking questions will help you accomplish your goals and feel good about yourself. You will gain insight, understanding, and skills that you can use in all areas of your life. Counselor should help students process their feelings regarding getting help, guiding them toward accepting the need for help as a positive instead of a negative. When a student shares his or her feelings, ask the class to give feedback. Allow adequate time for students to process, but try to stop 5–7 minutes prior to the end of the lesson. Let students know that they can continue their discussion next time.
6. End lesson by instructing students to turn over their Getting Help Worksheets to look at the five tips for Getting Help When You Need It. Read through each tip together, asking students to volunteer to read. Process each tip with the class.
7. Ask students to recall each tip.

Worksheet 7: Getting Help

Name:_____

Directions: Read Each Question Carefully, and Give the Answer That Describes You Best

1. I am comfortable asking a question in math class when I don't understand something.

   A = never true   B = sometimes true
   C = mostly true   D = always true

2. In math class there have been times when I have wanted to ask a question, but I don't.

   A = never true   B = sometimes true
   C = mostly true   D = always true

3. In math class, I don't like anyone to know if I don't understand something.

   A = never true   B = sometimes true
   C = mostly true   D = always true

4. In general, it's better to try to work on my own than to ask for help.

   A = never true   B = sometimes true
   C = mostly true   D = always true

5. When I ask for help, I ask questions that help me understand the material.

   A = never true   B = sometimes true
   C = mostly true   D = always true

6. When I ask for help, I just want to get the right answer so I can finish my assignment.

   A = never true   B = sometimes true
   C = mostly true   D = always true

7. At home, I can ask someone in my family for help if I don't understand how to do something.

   A = never true   B = sometimes true
   C = mostly true   D = always true

8. I give up if an assignment is too difficult to finish on my own.

   A = never true   B = sometimes true
   C = mostly true   D = always true

Tips for Getting Help When You Need It

- In class, never be afraid to ask a question. Questions help **everybody** understand things better! Try asking questions that begin with: "why?", "how?", or "what if?" Instead of just saying, "I don't understand." Remember to keep asking questions until you understand—you don't have to stop after asking once!
- Pay attention when other students ask questions. They might have the same question as you do! Also, hearing the answers to more questions will help you remember the material better.
- You can help yourself by "reflecting" on what you've already learned. Reflecting is when you ask yourself questions in order to help remember the material. You can do this by taking a practice test OR by trying to teach it to someone else (like a friend, brother, sister, mom, or dad).
- Ask for hints if you can do most of the problem but not all of it. A good question helps you get started when you are stuck—a bad question is to ask someone simply to do it for you.
- Read, think, then re-read the problem. If you are completely stuck on a problem, don't guess! Ask your teacher, "How do I start?"
- Always remember that getting help is an important part of learning. Knowing when and how to ask the right questions will help you reach your goals for the rest of your life!

Grade 6—Activity 8

Getting Help—The art of asking questions

Activity: Small group role-play. Divide class into small groups of 4–5 students. Each group gets a "problem-scenario" to read over. Groups must use their worksheets to describe the problem, the feelings/emotions of the person experiencing the problem, and possible questions to ask in order to get help solving the problem. Then, each group shares with the class and counselor facilitates discussion about asking questions.

Implementation time: 30 minutes

Materials: Getting Help Worksheet and example "problem-scenarios" for each group.

Objectives

Self-Efficacy Beliefs: Increase students' situational adaptivity. Increase students' self-reflection and metacognition as they learn to recognize the need for help. Reinforce students' ability to overcome threats to self-worth when asking for help, and increase feelings of autonomy through instrumental help-seeking behaviors.

Other Skills: Monitoring task performance and recognizing conceptual difficulties. Identifying skills, techniques, and strategies that can be applied to solve new problems. Recognizing different problems and when to ask for assistance during problem-solving.

Assessment

Participation in the small group role-play activity.

ASCA College- and Career Readiness Standard(s)

M 2.	Self-confidence in ability to succeed.
B-LS4.	Apply self-motivation and self-direction to learning
B-SMS 7.	Demonstrate effective coping skills when faced with a problem
B- SS 8.	Demonstrate advocacy skills and ability to assert self, when necessary

Lesson Plan: Getting Help—The art of asking questions

1. Begin lesson by asking students if they have any questions from last time. Allow for a few minutes of class discussion about getting help and the feelings they experience when asking questions.
2. Begin group activity by explaining to students that one of the best ways to learn how and when to ask the right question is to practice! Introduce the activity and explain the directions.
3. Place students into groups of 4–5 and give each group a copy of the Getting Help Worksheet. Give each group a "problem-scenario" and ask them to complete the worksheet. Allow 10–12 minutes for the activity.
4. When groups finish, ask each group to share their "problem-scenario" and the questions they created to help solve the problem. Counselor should facilitate the discussion by giving each group specific feedback about the questions they generated, emphasizing the importance of instrumental help-seeking behaviors. Examples are:

   - Not instrumental: "I don't understand"
   - Instrumental: "I don't understand why you did . . ."
   - Not instrumental: "Can you do problem 17?"
   - Instrumental: "Can you show me how to start problem 17?"

5. End the lesson with a class discussion on the importance of getting help when you need it. Counselor should validate help-seeking behaviors as an important strategy for managing the learning process. Distribute copies of the Help-Seeking Affirmations.

Possible "Problem-Scenarios"

- Gabriel missed a few days of school last week because he was sick. His parents picked up his homework for him, and he did most of it before coming back to school today. There were some things he didn't understand because he wasn't in class, and now he is even more behind today because the whole class has moved on to a new chapter.
- Amelia has always been really good at math and gets good grades. She got off to a good start this year, but lately, the class seems to be moving kind of fast, and everyone else seems to be understanding things better than she is. Sometimes her teacher skips steps when showing the class how to solve new problems.
- Antwan usually feels comfortable asking questions in class. Today, his teacher said something that he didn't understand, so he raised his hand and said, "I don't understand." When his teacher explained it again, Alex was still confused.
- Chen's class is learning to solve algebra equations. Rachel thought she understood everything the teacher covered last week, but when it came time to take the quiz, Rachel couldn't remember the steps and didn't do very well. The test is at the end of the week.

Worksheet 8: Getting Help Practice Worksheet
Name: _____

Directions: Read over your "problem-scenario" with your group, and answer the questions on the worksheet. Remember to use your "feeling" words to describe emotions.

1. What makes this situation a problem?

   _____
   _____
   _____
   _____
   _____

2. How do you think this person is feeling?

   _____
   _____
   _____
   _____
   _____

3.   What can this person do to solve the problem?

_____
_____
_____
_____
_____

Give one or two examples of questions this person can ask to get help.

_____
_____
_____
_____
_____
_____
_____

4   Using Claims and Evidence to Support the Search for Extraterrestrial Life

Teacher Reflections Following an Interdisciplinary English—Science Argumentation Unit

Ryan Summers, Kathy Rodems, Sharlene Denos, and Amy Atkinson

This We Believe Characteristics

- Educators value young adolescents and are prepared to teach them.
- Curriculum is challenging, exploratory, integrative, and relevant.
- A shared vision developed by all stakeholders guides every decision.

The *Next Generation Science Standards* identifies argumentation as a central practice, and, subsequently, energizes teachers to develop students' capacities to write well-reasoned arguments and support their claims with relevant evidence. These skills now expected in the science classroom have long been central to instruction in English language arts. This article overviews the design and delivery of a first-time interdisciplinary collaboration between three teachers, representing English-language arts, science, and a teacher-librarian. Their integrated unit was based on principles of scientific argumentation. Recounting the experience from the perspectives of the teachers, and informed by observations and interviews conducted, discussion centers on the practical aspects of unit delivery and meeting intended goals. This article thematically explores qualitative data collected from the teachers, including individual reflections and a focus group interview, as well as classroom observation and student post-unit survey data. Drawing on the experience from the inaugural implementation, we discuss considerations for future efforts and implications for the broader audience.

An interdisciplinary approach to curriculum gives equal attention to two or more disciplines and involves the explicit assimilation of concepts from the chosen areas (Drake & Burns, 2004). For more than 20 years, the Association for Middle-Level Education (formerly National Middle School Association) has promoted "integrative" curricula and advocated this approach in its books, journals, and national conference presentations (National Middle School Association, 2010). *Turning Points* 2000 (Jackson & Davis, 2000) called for integrating subject matter across disciplines, carrying the stance from the original *Turning Points* (Carnegie Council on Adolescent Development, 1989). The *Next Generation Science Standards* emphasized integrated, interdisciplinary instruction (NGSS; NGSS Lead States, 2013), which promotes intersections between science and other content areas, such as mathematics and English-language arts (e.g., Cheuk, 2016), as students interact with authentic questions, problems, and phenomena.

ARGUMENTATION: A PLATFORM FOR INTEGRATING ENGLISH AND SCIENCE INSTRUCTION

The *Framework for K-12 Science Education* (National Research Council [NRC], 2012), building on *Taking Science to School: Learning and Teaching Science in Grades K-8* (NRC, 2007) and the basis for the NGSS (NGSS Lead States, 2013), advocated the practice of scientific argument. Argument, in this sense, represents a complex form of reasoning that requires students to use science content knowledge and data or other evidence as the foundation for developing claims (NGSS Lead States, 2013). During this process, claims, or a proposed explanation, may be contested (Osborne & Patterson, 2011), and students may be required to defend their ideas, challenge alternatives, or revise their stances (Berland & Reiser, 2009). Argumentation and analysis that relate evidence to theory are essential features of science and the construction of scientific knowledge (McNeill & Krajcik, 2012); students, like scientists, need to be able to examine, review, and evaluate their own knowledge and ideas and critique those of others (NGSS Lead States, 2013, p. 27). Preparing students to participate in this vision of scientific argumentation requires they understand specific science topics (Osborne & Patterson, 2011) and be competent in retrieving and presenting meaningful evidence for the purpose of persuading an audience (Bybee, 2011). As such, this goal overlaps heavily with themes of argumentative writing and interaction with nonfiction text (Common Core State Standards Initiative, 2010). It is necessary to support students in learning how to participate in science discourse because the norms of scientific argument, explanation, and the evaluation of evidence differ from the strategies employed in everyday life (National Research Council, 2007, p. 186).

VIEWING THE LIBRARY AND LIBRARIAN AS RESOURCES

In recent years, school library educators and science educators have advocated for librarians to play a stronger role in science, primarily as teachers or instructional partners in facilitating the inquiry process in science, helping students understand science practices, and collaborating with science teachers to integrate different literacy practices (Mardis, 2006; Subramaniam et al., 2015). Guided by the principles set forth in the *Standards for the 21st Century Learner* issued by the American Association of School Librarians (AASL, 2007), teacher-librarians strive to embed research within a framework of authentic curiosity, guided discovery, and meaningful output, elevating traditional research to the realm of inquiry learning. This concept has a considerable history among school librarians that, for full realization, "needs to make its debut beyond school libraries within K-12 education" (Levitov, 2016). With their research expertise—a skill not typically taught in teacher education courses—teacher-librarians are valuable collaborators; as Maniotes and Kuhlthau (2014) noted, "school librarians can be leaders in inquiry learning because they know the research process and are able to help teachers design better learning experiences for students, experiences that support their learning through research" (p. 16). Research supporting this perspective indicated that science teachers may seek the help of school librarians to find reliable sources of information to supplement students' learning of content in the science classroom (Mardis & Hoffman, 2007; McIlvain, 2010; Pandora, 2009) and to locate novel and engaging instructional materials (McLean, 2010; Stewart, 2010; Subramaniam, Ahn, Fleischmann, & Druin, 2012). Transitioning to process-oriented approaches of knowledge acquisition and production, such as argumentation, demands strong ties between school librarians and classroom teachers from multiple disciplines to allow these methodologies to take root. School librarians, as described in the goals listed by Subramaniam et al. (2015), aim to promote reading as a foundational skill, and to teach inquiry and information skills as a means of helping students to thrive in complex learning environments. By cultivating other essential skills, such as technology literacy and critical thinking, librarians are well positioned to support student learning through scientific argumentation through the selection, use, creation, and evaluation of information.

Design and Implementation of the Integrated Argumentation Unit

The teachers involved in this project, Kathy Rodems, Sharlene Denos, and Amy Atkinson, designed and implemented an integrated scientific argumentation unit that centered on the topic of astro-biology.[1] Lessons in this unit were oriented in a project-based format, situating students as explorers on a NASA mission, as a means of enhancing student investment (Thomas, 2000). Through a series of activities completed in science and English classes, as well as the library, students tackled the driving question: Where might we find life outside of Earth in our solar system?

The activities in this unit were selected to guide students in developing a well-researched and defensible stance of where such an extraterrestrial search should be focused. The design of this unit allowed students to engage in hands-on inquiry activities in science to facilitate rich discussion on the possible habitability of planets, and/or moons, in our solar system. The measure of student learning for this five-week unit was a collaborative persuasive essay, referred to as the final argument task, requiring students to defend their choice of the most habitable planet or moon in our solar system. Each of the involved teachers assessed this final product independently according to criteria that aligned with their specific contributions.

Descriptions of key contributions from each of the three classrooms are presented in the three following paragraphs.

Sharlene—the science teacher—exposed students to a number of activities that connected requirements for life and habitability. These included a comparison of conditions found on each planet and moon as well as laboratory experiments that allowed students to determine the impact of such conditions (e.g., extremely acidic environments) on living cells. These activities were then connected to the major components of scientific argumentation using the claims-evidence-reasoning framework (Hillocks, 2011; McNeill & Krajcik, 2012) which is outlined with terms and definition in Table 4.1. Sharlene made explicit real-world connections to the concepts being addressed in her science class, and utilized examples of extreme habitats on Earth to enable students to establish a list of the minimum criteria for life. The focus of the unit, a project-based design with a challenge posed to students, along with the major science ideas explored in class prior to the development of their formal arguments is outlined in Figure 4.1. The science ideas and activities served to guide students to encounter central concepts and focused on a constructive investigation involving inquiry and knowledge building (Holm, 2011). Synthesizing the data collected across the various activities, students developed a ranked list of the most habitable places outside Earth in our solar system, a list that was later used as the foundation of their persuasive essays. Additionally, alongside the essay produced, students, in groups, participated in a culminating activity involving the real-time presentation of these arguments to demonstrate their ability to apply claims-evidence-reasoning (Figure 4.2). Coupling complex, integrated learning goals with a realistic product and presentation is a hallmark of the project-based instructional approach (Thomas, 2000).

Kathy—the English language arts teacher—previously introduced argument terms similar to those focused on in this unit when discussing short stories with her students. The components of a scientific argument—claim, evidence, reasoning, and rebuttal—were built upon throughout this integrated unit. Figure 4.3 provides a visual representation of these components, and examples collected from students' final

Challenge: You are leading a NASA team charged with hunting for life outside of Earth. You decide to start with our own solar system, but because it is so vast, your only hope of succeeding is if you target your search to the most likely places where you might find living things. As you start to create your plan you realize you're not sure what living things need to survive or even what it means to be living!

(Students investigated this issue, outlined in the three parts below, before going on to build their argument nominating a planet or moon that could support life – e.g., Titan, Mars, Venus, Enceladus, Io, or Europa.)

Part 1: Background
A. Discuss what distinguishes living from non-living. Consider the following examples: DNA, seeds, viruses, yeast, a single cell, and fire.

B. Based on your discussion create a description and heuristic useful for distinguishing between living and non-living.

C. List factors that may limit or prevent the growth of living organisms.

Part 2: Research and Investigate
A. Become familiar with extremophile habitats, beginning with the resources provided. Work to compile information about what makes each habitat seem inhospitable for life.

B. Further explore how each of these extreme environments might impact cells by conducting a protein denaturation lab.

Part 3: Synthesize
A. Revise your list of factors that may limit or prevent life following your investigation of extremophile habitats and organisms,

B. Develop a list of tolerances for each factor you list. For example, if you list temperature as an important factor then include a range of temperatures that can support life and mention specific organisms that can survive at the extremes.

Figure 4.1 Overview of Major Science Ideas Explored in This Unit Prior to Argument Development

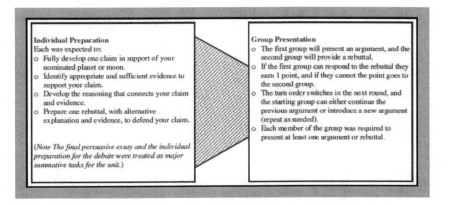

Figure 4.2 Student Preparation and Group Presentation Format for the Culminating Debate Activity in the Argumentation Unit

argument are included in Table 4.1. For her contribution, Kathy placed a strong emphasis on helping students to identify and understand these components for the benefit of their own writing and to dismantle primary literature articles. Over the course of this unit, Kathy helped the students

Table 4.1 Claims, Evidence, Reasoning, and Rebuttals Explained and Contextualized

Component	Definition[a]	Example in this context[b]
Claim	A statement that expresses the answer or conclusion to a question or problem (p. 22).	The second important criterion to look for is energy, which is essential to sustaining life. . . . On Europa, there are quite a few different sources that could provide energy which makes it extremely likely that life could exist there (p. 5).
Evidence	Evidence is scientific data that supports the claim (p. 23). Data includes information from observations and measurements and also from secondhand sources.	Jupiter's gravity is slightly stronger on the near side of Europa than on the far side, and the magnitude of this difference changes as Europa orbits, which causes the tides that stretch and relax Europa's surface. . . . [C]ontinuous flexing creates heat, which makes Europa's interior warm (pp. 5–6).
Reasoning	The reasoning explains why the evidence supports the claim, providing a logical connection between the evidence and the claim (p. 24).	Because of this heat, below the thick layer of ice, there is an ocean of liquid water where life could exist. . . . The tidal heating is what keeps Europa's ocean liquid and could prove critical to the survival of organisms within the ocean. . . . This heat can also be a source of energy to any life in the water (p. 6).
Rebuttal	The rebuttal recognizes and describes alternative explanations and provides counter evidence and reasoning for why the alternative explanation is not the appropriate explanation for the question or problem (p. 25)	Some critics may argue that the water on Europa can be too acidic for it to sustain life. . . . Even though the ocean might be acidic, there are extremophiles that have lived in the pH of 0.0, which is the pH rating of battery acid (p. 5).

a See McNeill and Krajcik (2012) for discussion of terms and definitions.
b Select examples from Student Group #2 Final Argument.

write several arguments that began as simple and progressed to complex. Once the final assignment was given, Kathy assisted the students in finding, comprehending, and documenting resources, crafting the individual and group components of the argument, conducting peer review, and aiding with formatting and other general writing-related needs. Keeping in line with the goal of the unit, Kathy utilized five large tablets that were capable of supporting multiple users simultaneously (Lenovo *Horizon* multi-touch surfaces) to promote group work and collaboration.

Amy—as teacher-librarian—contributed to the project in four key ways: the identification of resources for the classroom teachers, the instruction

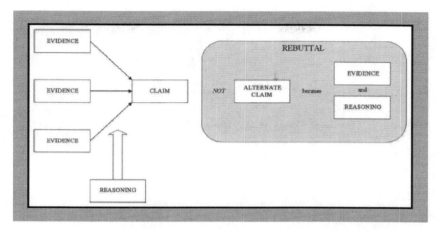

Figure 4.3 Overview of Claim, Evidence, Reasoning, and Rebuttal Framework
Source: (adapted from McNeill & Krajcik, 2012)

of students in article discovery and retrieval, instruction of students in understanding and creation of abstracts, and instruction of students in APA citation formatting. Determination of these contributions emerged from ongoing conversations between Amy and the two classroom teachers, and evolved along with the parameters of the project. The convergence of standards-based practices from the core disciplines on argumentation, drawing from NGSS and CCSS, are summarized in Figure 4.4. These practices are complemented by a list of exemplar AASL standards outlined by Amy as intended learning for students. The AASL standards that mirrored the other areas are listed below:

1.1.3. Develop and refine a range of questions to frame the search for new understanding.
1.1.5. Evaluate information found in selected sources on the basis of accuracy, validity, appropriateness for needs, importance, and social and cultural context.
2.1.1. Continue an inquiry-based research process by applying critical-thinking skills (analysis, synthesis, evaluation, organization) to information and knowledge to construct new understandings, draw conclusions, and create new knowledge.

Learning Environment and Student Participants

The school wherein the argumentation unit was enacted is a selective admission, public, state-sanctioned laboratory school affiliated with a

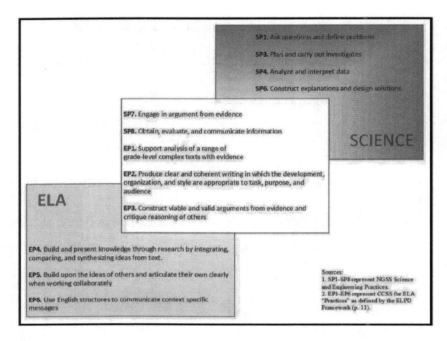

Figure 4.4 Relationships and Convergences Between ELA and Science Practices in Supporting Argumentation

Source: (Adapted from Cheuk, 2016, p. 94)

large university in the Midwest.[2] The school serves academically talented students at the middle (combined Grades 7 and 8) and high school levels (Grades 9–12). A total of 65 students, representing all students in the combined seventh- and eighth-grade level, participated in the integrated unit activities during the fall of 2015. It is important to underscore there is considerable cultural and ethnic diversity among the students even though admission to the school is selective. In addition, it is worth mentioning that the school, although publicly funded, it is not tied to a school district. Teachers in this setting have considerable freedom to experiment with learning strategies and curriculum. Instructional flexibility combined with the high disciplinary content knowledge of the teaching faculty, many of whom hold advanced or terminal degrees in their content areas, makes this setting ideal for delivering integrative units.

Data Sources and Analysis

Different and equally important data sources were *intentionally* used in an aim to get a better insight into teachers' overall experience with the integrated unit. Following the delivery of the unit, teachers individually completed reflection questions, allowing them to express their views and experiences with the design and implementation (see Appendix A). Teachers later participated in a focus group interview, targeting *the same questions*, which provided an opportunity for them to share and elaborate on their individual reflections, and discuss these issues collectively (Shotland & Mark, 1987). The researcher who moderated the focus group was not involved with the design or delivery of the unit. With less involvement, this researcher needed to know more information about the practices that were going on in the class, and pressed teachers to explain details related to the implementation of the unit. To allow for the triangulation of the data, a second researcher observed and analyzed classroom instruction at the three classrooms. This observer had an idea of what was going on in the unit, and—though he did not engage in classroom activities—the teachers were comfortable with his presence in class. His role was to record notes on the classroom dynamics and the way the technologies were being used. Additionally, to illuminate and substantiate issues raised by the teachers, final student products and responses to select questions from a post-unit survey completed by students were reviewed. In summary, the major source of data came from the teachers' responses to post-unit reflection questions and group interview discussion, supplemented by classroom observation and student survey data. Analysis of the qualitative data from the above sources converged on three main themes related to the implementation of the integrated unit. They are presented in the following sections.

Teacher Growth and Collaboration Across Disciplines

All the teachers involved, through the reflection questionnaires and the focus group interview, spoke about the fit of the teachers involved and how they were able to accomplish this unit by drawing on the strengths of their collaborators. In general, Sharlene functioned as the content expert for the science-related theme of the unit, and she assisted the other teachers by articulating examples and principles. Still, reflecting on her thoughts from the onset of this project, Sharlene noted that she would have been uncomfortable developing the argumentation unit on her own. Kathy went on to explain in her reflection how different this experience was at multiple stages from her typical practice, stating:

> . . . [T]he way I prepared for this project was very different. I typically rely on previous knowledge, online resources, or a collection of books and manuals that I have in my office to prepare for the lessons. For this assignment, I observed S's science class for a week to have a better understanding of the scientific principles and concepts.

While Kathy admitted in a later question how this experience reminded her of how long it had been since she last received science instruction, she vocalized a number of benefits that this experience brought to her own classroom teaching. She went on to highlight how the inquiry activities that she observed in Sharlene's class helped her to plan and anchor accompanying instruction:

> I feel that observing Sharlene's class has made a significant impact on the information that I provided for the students. Our focus for the project [was] on scientific arguments and explanations. After giving the students the definitions for these categories (claim, evidence, reasoning, rebuttal), I was able to use the actual labs they performed as examples for each category. I think these authentic examples have made a substantial impact on my own understanding of the concepts and how best to convey the information to the students therefore creating more concrete and accurate in-class discussions of the scientific explanations.

In the focus group Sharlene, who had talked to Kathy about the observation experience, reported that she was eager to participate in peer observation in the future. All the teachers went on to say that implementing the integrated unit was, overall, a positive experience. They also expressed a willingness to consider teaching more integrated units and potentially recruiting more teachers from other disciplines in the future.

For Amy, communication, receptiveness, responsiveness, and knowledge of relevant resources proved key. Building this project from the ground up required a good deal of back-and-forth not only to lay the groundwork for the unit but also to refine the resources cultivated for certain elements of the project. After initial meetings of the three teachers, Amy mined various relevant databases available through the library for writing samples that made scientific arguments using accessible language. The three teachers then refined this selection based on the developing scope of the project, ultimately leading to the selection of Pro/Con articles from *The CQ Researcher* that exemplified the argument/rebuttal format targeted at a young audience. Amy also reported that ongoing conversations with Sharlene and Kathy helped her to focus classroom instruction portions of the unit by increasing her understanding of the students' abilities and needs, thus enabling her to help students grow their own knowledge through principles of guided inquiry. Finally, once the teaching team decided upon the final assessment structure, Amy used her own Information Literacy class to prepare the students, instituting a mock trial in which students examined and adjudicated various scenarios involving ethical dilemmas, thereby practicing the critical thinking and public speaking skills needed for the interdisciplinary project's culminating debates. By staying in communication with Sharlene and Kathy and being receptive to the changes of the unit and responsive to the shifting needs, Amy was able to help the students with their own information seeking, interpretation, and synthesis.

Students' Perception of Integrated Instruction

Students offered a number of positive comments about the integrated nature of the unit when asked "What activities and aspects led to collaboration, communication, and the most learning?" One student stated in their post-unit survey "I feel like . . . having time in both science and English to work on this unit led to positive collaboration, communication, and the most learning." From the perspective of the teacher, Sharlene voiced her observations about student engagement with the unit explaining:

> I think the value of this project is in the quality of the lessons created by content experts in each discipline and in the way it has been fully integrated into each class. Students have moved seamlessly from collecting and analyzing scientific data to constructing arguments and writing and then back to thinking about data almost as though there were no such thing as separate science and English classes.

It is important to note that students ultimately composed their final argument with the groups set in their English class. The structure of the school and schedule, more typical of a junior high or high school setting as judged by a "well-entrenched departmentalized structure" (Kasak & Uskali, 2012, p. 129), made it so that students were not in the same group for both English and science class. Students commented that it was helpful to be able to communicate with your group members daily, but there may have been some unplanned advantages with this arrangement. One student commented on the benefit, from their perspective, in being required to work and interact with different groups in each class, as opposed to static groups, saying:

> Having to write the paper with a group, especially with a group that wasn't the same as the one in science, definitely made it so that we had to learn to communicate with each other, because we all had different ideas, and we had to learn to compromise.
>
> (Anonymous student, post-unit survey)

Regarding the collaborative focus of the unit in their responses to post-unit survey questions ("Could you have learned as much if you had done this by yourself or was there value added from collaborating with peers?"), many students commented that they learned more than they thought they would have if working alone. One student stated, "I think

I learned more than if I had worked on my own. The others on my team had some different points that I hadn't thought of, and the debate also brought up really well thought out arguments too." Exposure to multiple viewpoints, through group work and collaboration, may have enabled students to more readily predict and refute counterarguments as some students suggested in their survey responses. Further, advocates of project-based learning have argued that students benefit from increased problem-solving and collaboration skills compared to traditional forms of instruction (Holm, 2011).

Teachers' Views on the Effectiveness of Technology

The most frequent finding across responses to teachers' reflections, the focus group, and observations from the classroom was the positive view of the importance of technology, specifically the multi-touch tablets, in teaching this unit. Following teachers' concordant beliefs about the usefulness of the technologies in their classes, the second most frequent finding among the three data sources was that technologies were helpful for the students. Other prevalent teachers' views included the effect of these technologies on the nature and degree of engagement in their classrooms. When prompted, all teachers, in at least one of the data sources, expressed excitement and determination is using these technologies in the future.

In general, the teachers viewed their classrooms as being more student-centered, and more accommodating of collaboration during the implementation of this unit compared to their typical instruction. An individual reflection response from Kathy highlights the role of technology in facilitating collaboration and her hopes for using the large multi-touch tablets compared to a more typical scenario involving laptops for writing activities. She stated:

> [S]tudents used the Lenovo tablets to craft the introduction and conclusion to the group essays. I think that if the students were assigned this portion of the assignment with regular laptops, then I am afraid they would not collaboratively write these portions—they would each take a portion and write individually.

In an observation of one of Kathy's classes, a similar situation manifested and was documented. The researcher noted a lower student engagement for a particular class period. It seemed to stem from the choice of two groups of students who had elected to use laptops instead of the large multi-touch tablets. The researcher noted, "The students who were working in groups without the tablets were noticeably less engaged in group-level or class discussion." When informally asked about their choice to use laptops for the writing activity that day instead of the tablets by the researcher in the classroom, the students contended they could get more done by working on separate portions. Kathy, when asked about the incident and the group involved, acknowledged that there was a strong "divide and conquer" approach too that she felt was likely to have been instilled through more traditional instruction methods. This finding substantiates the views of the teachers regarding the importance of student collaboration while also serving as an example of how student choice and engagement with particular technology could impact the outcomes observed. When recounting this event during the teacher group interview, Kathy stated that she believed the tablets improved the peer writing process. She noted that the tablets improved student discussion during the peer review in her classroom, explaining:

> If students are simply given an essay and a set of questions to answer, the process becomes very critical, static, and author and peer reviewer messages can be misunderstood. Using the tablets to peer review allowed the students to have a dialogue about the essay, which essentially helps them work through some of the traditional peer review issues.

Teachers' Perspective: Lessons Learned and Thoughts About Future Designs

Reflecting on the interdisciplinary argumentation unit, and planning for the future, the teachers ultimately determined that the topic was too limited and did not provide opportunities for students to develop complex and distinct arguments. Indeed, the primary complaint from teachers involved was how tedious it was to read students' papers because of their lack of original ideas and repetitive argument structure. Students' nominations illustrated this concern with 14 of the 20 final projects championing either Enceladus or Europa as a potential host of life, and with similar evidence presented in arguing for the viability of their chosen location. However, even when connected to a narrow topic, the teachers discovered during the evaluation of the projects that it was still possible for students to produce a well-written essay that did not support scientific claims with appropriate evidence. In many cases, the strongest essays in either content area were judged to be above average overall, but one group out of the 20 did very well on the English component and was judged poor in science content. This situation, while rare, further highlights the value of interdisciplinary collaboration and utilizing the content expertise of different teachers.

Since the implementation of this argumentation unit, the teachers have opted to anchor future instruction involving interdisciplinary units around socioscientific issues. Socioscientific issues are based on authentic and contemporary problems facing society and provide students an opportunity to explore and develop complex arguments for topics in which there is no "correct" answer (for additional reading, see Kinslow & Sadler, 2018). Often these, issues are complicated from a scientific perspective with conflicting pieces of information as well as social considerations, and can be made to connect with issues present in the local community of which the school is a part. As word about this collaboration spread across the school, the number of other potential teacher-collaborators from various other disciplines who wanted to participate amazed the teachers. Sharlene reported that the current iteration of the collaboration, which now also includes a social studies teacher, centers on issues of water supply and contaminants, including those that have no safe minimum level for certain vulnerable populations (e.g., lead). The crisis in Flint, Michigan, serving as a real-world example, provided a natural segue to science content including the chemistry of corrosion in lead pipes, the neuropathology of lead poisoning, water testing, and the concept of fair tests in making data-driven decisions.

Rich ethical issues in relation to recent cases of elevated lead levels in municipal water systems, draws attention to significant racial and socio-economic disparities that may exist in exposure to these toxins through the water supply. This scenario also provides a rich context to facilitate student argumentation by asking students to propose strategies for monitoring and mitigation of lead risks in drinking water or a cost-benefit analysis when there are real limits on what cities can pay to purify water. To capitalize on the complexity of this scenario, the teachers opted to expand the scope of the unit to include political and moral dimensions in addition to arguments grounded in science and empirical data.

Implications for Fellow Educators

A clear message from the testimony of the teachers involved in the argumentation unit with implications for others who are interested in pursuing new, interdisciplinary collaborations relates to the fit—or, rather the relationship, willingness to collaborate, trust, and collegiality of the individuals involved (Fairman & Mackenzie, 2015). In addition to unique and complementary expertise, the teachers involved in this project all wanted to see this integrated unit succeed. Vangrieken, Dochy, Raes, and Kyndt (2015) draw attention to the shared motivation and commitment resulting from teacher collaboration in their systematic review of studies (n = 82). In this case, while designing and delivering the argumentation unit, the teaching team assumed a joint responsibility for the planning, teaching, and assessing the progress of all students (Villa, Thousand, & Nevin, 2008). This cohesive approach may have fostered some of the affective outcomes reported by the teachers (Egodawatte, McDougall, & Stoilescu, 2011).

More specifically, two of our authors (Kathy and Amy) were highly flexible with their teaching schedule to facilitate connections with the science content throughout the unit. Main and Bryer (2005) noted that this flexibility enables fruitful teacher collaboration. It is critical to highlight the teachers were able to function in this way even though they were in a school with a departmental structure that did not naturally encourage interdisciplinary collaborations. Research has shown that teacher collaboration can affect student learning (e.g., Main & Bryer, 2005), but opportunities and support for collaboration can be influenced by school leadership (Leithwood & Jantzi, 2008). Over the course of this unit, the teachers recognized that the support they received from their administrators and fellow teachers was critical to their success (e.g., providing substitutes to allow for shared planning time and peer observation time, and allowing classes to be moved to accommodate the combined Science-English argument presentation task). Teacher collaborations may not come as naturally as it did for the teachers involved in this project, but their story should be an example for other practitioners about the rewarding interdisciplinary learning opportunities that can be created in middle-level classrooms.

Notes

1. National Aeronautics and Space Administration (2006) and NOVA (2012) include helpful resources that were adapted as parts of this unit to address astro-biology as described.
2. Laboratory schools flourished in the United States between the mid-19th and 20th centuries. Typically affiliated with university and college campuses, these schools have played a major role in educational research and teacher preparation. One of the most famous schools was founded in 1894 in Chicago by the psychologist and philosopher John Dewey. Many of these schools distinguish themselves today by their use of existing and new research findings to inform their programmatic choices (Haag, 2017).

References

American Association of School Librarians. (2007). *AASL standards for the 21st-century learner*. Retrieved from www.ala.org/aasl/standards

Berland, L. K., & Reiser, B. J. (2009). Making sense of argumentation and explanation. *Science Education, 93*(1), 26–55. https://doi.org/10.1002/sce.v93:1

Bybee, R. W. (2011). Scientific and engineering practices in K-12 classrooms. *The Science Teacher, 78*(9), 34–40.

Carnegie Council on Adolescent Development. (1989). *Turning points: Preparing American youth for the 21st century*. New York: Carnegie Corporation.

Cheuk, T. (2016). Discourse practices in the new standards: The role of argumentation in common core-era next generation science standards classrooms for English language arts learners. *Electronic Journal of Science Education, 20*(3), 92–111.

Common Core State Standards Initiative. (2010). *Common core state standards for English language arts & literacy in history/social studies, science, and technical subjects.* Washington, DC: National Governors Association for Best Practices and Council of Chief State School Officers.

Drake, S. M., & Burns, R. C. (2004). *Meeting standards through integrated curriculum.* Alexandria, VA: Association for Supervision and Curriculum Development.

Egodawatte, G., McDougall, D., & Stoilescu, D. (2011). The effects of teacher collaboration in grade 9 applied mathematics. *Educational Research for Policy and Practice, 10*(3), 189–209. https://doi.org/10.1007/s10671-011-9104-y

Fairman, J. C., & Mackenzie, S. V. (2015). How teacher leaders influence others and understand their leadership. *International Journal of Leadership in Education, 18*(1), 61–87. https://doi.org/10.1080/13603124.2014.904002

Haag, P. (2017). Laboratory schools: A new educational phenomenon. *The Conversation.* Retrieved from https://theconversation.com/laboratory-schools-a-new-educational-phenomenon-79071

Hillocks, G., Jr. (2011). *Teaching argument writing.* Portsmouth, NH: Heinemann.

Holm, M. (2011). Project-based instruction: A review of the literature on effectiveness in prekindergarten through 12th grade classrooms. *Rivier Academic Journal, 7*(2), 1–13.

Jackson, A., & Davis, G. A. (2000). *Turning points 2000: Educating adolescents in the 21st century.* New York: Teachers College Press.

Kasak, D., & Uskali, E. (2012). Organizational structures: Organizational structures foster purposeful learning and meaningful relationships. In *This we believe in action: Implementing successful middle schools* (pp. 119–131). Westerville, OH: Association for Middle Level Education.

Kinslow, A. T., & Sadler, T. (2018). Making science relevant: Using socio-scientific issues to foster critical thinking. *The Science Teacher, 86*(1), 40–45. https://doi.org/10.2505/4/tst18_086_01_40

Leithwood, K., & Jantzi, D. (2008). Linking leadership to student learning: The contributions of leader efficacy. *Educational Administration Quarterly, 44*(4), 496–528. https://doi.org/10.1177/0013161X08321501

Levitov, D. (2016). School libraries, librarians, and inquiry learning. *Teacher Librarian, 43*(3), 28.

Main, K., & Bryer, F. (2005). What does a "good" teaching team look like in a middle school classroom? In B. Bartlett, F. Bryer, & D. Roebouck (Eds.), *Stimulating the "action" as participants in participatory research: Proceedings of the 3rd International Conference on Cognition, Language, and Special Education.* Brisbane, Australia: Griffith University. Retrieved from www98.griffith.edu.au/dspace/handle/10072/2538

Maniotes, L., & Kuhlthau, C. (2014). The shift from traditional research to guided inquiry learning. *Knowledge Quest, 43*(2), 9–17.

Mardis, M. A. (2006). Science teacher and school library media specialist roles: Mutually reinforcing perspectives as defined by national guidelines. In M. Orey, V. J. McClendon, & R. B. Branch (Eds.), *Educational media and technology yearbook* (Vol. 31, pp. 169–178). Westport, CT: Libraries Unlimited.

Mardis, M. A., & Hoffman, E. (2007). Collection and collaboration: Science in Michigan middle school media centers. *School Library Media Research, 10*.

Retrieved from www.ala.org/aasl/aaslpubsandjournals/slmrb/slmrcontents/volume10/mardis_collectionandcollaboration

McIlvain, E. (2010). NSDL as a teacher empower point. *Knowledge Quest, 39*(2), 54–63.

McLean, L. (2010). Cook up with curriculum with content clips. *Knowledge Quest, 39*(2), 40–47.

McNeill, K. L., & Krajcik, J. S. (2012). *Supporting grade 5–8 students in constructing explanations in science: The claim, evidence, and reasoning framework for talk and writing.* Boston, MA: Pearson.

National Aeronautics and Space Administration. (2006). *Astrobiology in your classroom: Life on earth. . . . and elsewhere, version 2.0* [PDF file]. Retrieved from https://nai.nasa.gov/media/medialibrary/2013/10/Astrobiology-Educator-Guide-2007.pdf

National Middle School Association. (2010). *This we believe: Keys to educating young adolescents.* Westerville, OH: Author.

National Research Council. (2007). *Taking science to school: Learning and teaching science in grades K-8* (R. A. Duschl, H. A. Schweingruber, & A. W. Shouse, Eds.). Committee on Science Learning, Kindergarten Through Eighth Grade. Board on Science Education, Center for Education. Division of Behavioral and Social Sciences and Education. Washington, DC: The National Academies Press.

National Research Council. (2012). *A framework for K-12 science education: Practices, crosscutting concepts, and core ideas.* Washington, DC: National Academies Press.

NGSS Lead States. (2013). *Next generation science standards: For states, by states.* Washington, DC: National Academies Press. Retrieved from www.nextgenscience.org/next-generation-science-standards

NOVA. (2012). *Finding life beyond earth* [Video files]. Retrieved from www.pbs.org/wgbh/nova/education/space/finding-life-beyond-earth-collection.html#video

Osborne, J. F., & Patterson, A. (2011). Scientific argument and explanation: A necessary distinction? *Science Education, 95*(4), 627–638. https://doi.org/10.1002/sce.20438

Pandora, C. (2009). STEM—How libraries provide STEM information. *Ohio Media Spectrum, 61*(1), 23–27.

Shotland, R. L., & Mark, M. M. (1987). Improving inferences from multiple methods. In M. M. Mark & R. L. Shotland (Eds.), *Multiple methods in program evaluation: New directions for program evaluation* (pp. 77–94). San Francisco, CA: Jossey-Bass.

Stewart, M. (2010). Bringing science to life with readers' theater. *Knowledge Quest, 39*(2), 107–109.

Subramaniam, M., Ahn, J., Fleischmann, K. R., & Druin, A. (2012). Reimagining the role of school libraries in STEM education: Creating hybrid spaces for exploration. *Library Quarterly, 82*(2), 161–182. https://doi.org/10.1086/664578

Subramaniam, M., Ahn, J., Waugh, A., Taylor, N. G., Druin, A., Fleischmann, K. R., & Walsh, G. (2015). The role of school librarians in enhancing science learning. *Journal of Librarianship and Information Science, 47*(1), 3–16. https://doi.org/10.1177/0961000613493920

Thomas, J. W. (2000). *A review of research on PBL* [PDF file]. Retrieved from www.bobpearlman.org/BestPractices/PBL_Research.pdf

Vangrieken, K., Dochy, F., Raes, E., & Kyndt, E. (2015). Teacher collaboration: A systematic review. *Educational Research Review*, *15*, 17–40. https://doi.org/10.1016/j.edurev.2015.04.002

Villa, R. A., Thousand, J. S., & Nevin, A. (2008). *A guide to coteaching: Practical tips for facilitating student learning*. Thousand Oaks, CA: Corwin Press.

Appendix A
Teacher Reflection Questionnaire

[Teachers were asked to respond to the following prompts, and then bring their composed responses to the final focus group meeting following the delivery of the unit.]

1. In what ways, if any, did your teaching strategies deviate from normal for the purpose of this project?
2. If you did change your teaching strategy for the purpose of this project:

   a. Do you feel these changes were effective?
   b. Can you see yourself incorporating any of these strategies in the future, for other classes or other grade levels? If yes, please describe how.

3. How comfortable were you with integrating other topics (social sciences, science math, English, etc.) that may have not been in your field of expertise?

   a. What kinds of difficulties did you face when writing your lesson plans?
   b. Comment on the nature of support that you got for planning your lessons. Did you find working with other teachers in your school to be helpful?
   c. Do you think the integrated lesson plans were well received by students? Were there noticeable changes in their attention or interest in the lessons?
   d. As a result of this project do you feel more confident in integrating more than one topic in your future teaching?

4. In what ways were the instructional technologies you used helpful in facilitating the lessons associated with this project?

   a. In what ways do you think those instructional technologies allowed you to do things that you could not have done without?

    b.   Knowing that your school gets to keep the technologies, in what ways do you think you are going to use them after the project is over?

5. Comment on the science and English-language arts coordinated instruction utilized during this project. Had you done this kind of cooperative teaching before? Is this something you are more willing to explore in the future as a result of your experiences with this project?

Section II

Middle-Level Teacher Preparation

5 Interdisciplinary Curriculum

Using Poetry to Integrate Reading and Writing Across the Curriculum

William P. Bintz and Gumiko Monobe

This We Believe Characteristics

- Students and teachers are engaged in active, purposeful learning.
- Curriculum is challenging, exploratory, integrative, and relevant.

> *I teach reading and writing separately. Common Core State Standards, however, expect teachers to integrate reading writing. I also teach content areas separately. I have science time and social studies time. I want to integrate my content areas, too, because CCSS also expects teachers to use literacy to teach science and social studies. I want to know how to integrate reading, writing, and the content areas.*
>
> (6th grade teacher)

Statements like this are often shared by middle-level preservice and in-service teachers. This article was inspired by these teacher voices and shares results from a collaborative, classroom-based, research project conducted by two teacher educators who used an instructional strategy, centered on poetry, with in-service, graduate education students from multiple content areas. The purpose of this strategy was for students to actively experience interdisciplinary curriculum using poetry to integrate reading and writing across the curriculum and thoughtfully reflect on the benefits of interdisciplinary curriculum for students and teachers. We designed this strategy to reflect several characteristics of successful schools according to *This We Believe: Keys to Educating Young Adolescents* (The Association for Middle-Level Education (formerly National Middle School Association)) (NMSA, 2010). These characteristics are based in the area of Curriculum, Instruction, and Assessment and include that students and teachers are engaged in active, purposeful learning, and that curriculum is challenging, exploratory, integrative, and relevant.

We begin by describing the importance of integrated curriculum and highlighting the metaphorical tug-of-war that currently exists between interdisciplinary and disciplinary views of curriculum. Next, we provide the theoretical lens through which this research project was developed and implemented, including a rationale for why teacher research is important at all grade levels and how developing, implementing, and reflecting on integrated curriculum benefits middle-level students and teachers in numerous and complex ways. Then, we provide an overview of the research project and describe an instructional strategy, centered on poetry, that we presented to graduate students from multiple content areas. The purpose of this strategy was for students to actively experience using poetry to integrate reading and writing across the curriculum and thoughtfully reflect on the power and potential of interdisciplinary curriculum. Afterwards, we share samples of poems from different content areas that resulted from this instructional strategy and student reflections on the integrated experience. We end with lessons learned and pose next steps.

Importance of Integrated Curriculum

Integrated curriculum has a long and rich intellectual history. In the late twentieth century, John Dewey (1910) noted that integrated learning was inherently natural to learners and challenged the notion of a departmentalized view of learning. He argued that separating and isolating content areas in the school curriculum was arbitrary and blurred the natural relationships content areas have with each other. He stated:

> In the first place, there is no line of demarcation within facts themselves, which classifies them as belonging to science, history, or geography, respectively. The pigeon-hole classification which is so prevalent at present (fostered by introducing the pupil at the outset into a number of different studies contained in different textbooks) gives an utterly erroneous idea of the relations of studies to one another and to the intellectual whole to which all belong. In fact, these subjects have to do with the same ultimate reality, namely, the conscious experience of man. It is only because we have different interests, or different ends, that we sort out the material and label part of it science, part of it history, part geography, and so on.
>
> (p. 7)

Since then, the popularity of interdisciplinary curriculum has increased and decreased over the years. More recently, interest in interdisciplinary curriculum and integrated teaching and learning have once again received favorable attention in the United States as an alternative to a separate subject curriculum (Akins & Akerson, 2002; Weinberg & Sample McMeeking, 2017). This interest has been voiced by teacher educators and driven by a search for a new "coherence and integrity in the teacher education curriculum" (Fang & Ashley, 2004, p. 39). Teacher educators now recommend that preservice teachers acquire knowledge of interdisciplinary curriculum and abilities to organize academic disciplines around broad, interdisciplinary, themed topics of study (Heimer & Winokur, 2015; Richards & Shea, 2006).

Many professional organizations and much professional literature continue to express interest in and document the benefits of interdisciplinary curriculum. The International Reading Association (IRA), National Council for Teachers of English (NCTE), National Council of Teachers of Mathematics (NCTM), National Council of Social Studies (NCSS), and National Science Teachers Association (NSTA) all promote interdisciplinary curriculum and demonstrate that good things happen when teachers integrate the curriculum. Integrating science and literacy is a good example.

NSTA often publishes themed issues in their journals, *Science and Children, Science Scope,* and *The Science Teacher* on integrating science and literacy, as well as publishes a regular column on "Teaching Science Through Trade Books" (Bintz & Moore, 2005). This professional literature indicates that when instructional time is used to integrate science and literacy, student achievement in science is at significantly higher levels than when the two subjects are taught separately (Romance & Vitale, 1992). Moreover, research indicates that when science and reading are integrated, reading achievement scores improve as well (Royce & Wiley, 2005).

Today, the importance of interdisciplinary curriculum is best illustrated in the widespread interest in STEM, a common abbreviation used for four interrelated disciplines: Science, Technology, Engineering, and Mathematics. Science and mathematics are familiar disciplines, but technology and engineering are less so. Technology is defined as "the innovation, change, or modification of the natural environment in order to satisfy perceived human wants and needs" (ITEEA, 2000, p. 242). The engineering design cycle is the thinking process engineers use to solve problems and can be used as an organizing idea for instruction which focuses on integrating the STEM disciplines (see Lachapelle, Sargianis, & Cunningham, 2013; Morgan & Ansberry, 2015). While engineering is sometimes described as an invisible profession, it is at the core of STEM understanding and STEM thinking. Such thinking is important for us to use as literate members of society when we make important decisions (e.g., healthcare decisions or voting on environmental issues). STEM thinking is also equally important in many of the twenty-first century's fastest growing career fields.

At the same time, it is important to recognize that a metaphorical tug-of-war exists between interdisciplinary and disciplinary curriculum. On the one hand, an interdisciplinary view of curriculum posits that students (and teachers) live in an integrated world and think in integrated ways outside of school. Therefore, the curriculum in school should reflect the integrated world outside of school. This means that content areas are integrated across the curriculum, not taught separately. On the other hand, a disciplinary view of curriculum posits that content area material is best taught and learned separately, not integratedly, and that focusing on content areas one at a time is more efficient and effective.

The reality is that a disciplinary view of curriculum has been, and continues to be, quite popular in schools K-16. In the primary grades, students are in one class and with one teacher, but the day is still organized around separate subjects—e.g., reading time, math time, etc. In the upper grades, students move from class to class, teacher to teacher, subject to subject. Teacher education is no different. It continues to be based on a disciplinary view of curriculum. Preservice and in-service teachers move from course to course, professor to professor, and semester to semester, often taking courses that are content area specific (e.g., reading methods, math methods, science methods, etc.).

As literacy education professors, we teach courses that are fundamentally based on a disciplinary view of curriculum and promote the notion of teachers as researchers. Our goal, however, is to include both disciplinary and interdisciplinary experiences for our preservice and in-service students, and to situate our students and ourselves as teacher researchers. We do both by conducting classroom-based research projects that highlight interdisciplinary curriculum and invite our students to participate as our collaborators. Ultimately, when it comes to integrated curriculum, our goal is not to preach but to practice what we preach.

Theoretical Lens

Research is critically important to teaching. In fact, the existence and primacy of research is what makes teaching an academic profession, rather than a para-profession, unskilled job, or even a hobby. Researchers conduct research in order to build an extensive body of knowledge that teachers can use to make informed curricular, instructional, and evaluative decisions in the classroom. Researchers conduct educational research in many different ways (experimental, quasi-experimental, mixed-method, survey, questionnaire, interpretive, etc.) and across many different contexts (countries, laboratories, classrooms, internet, etc.).

Importance of Teacher Research

Teacher research is very important. In fact, Stenhouse (1983) asserts that it is difficult to see how teaching can be improved without research on the part of teachers. Therefore, in addition to including interdisciplinary and disciplinary experiences for our students, we used teacher research as the theoretical lens to conduct this research project. Teacher research is "systematic and intentional inquiry carried out by teachers" (Cochran-Smith & Lytle, 1992, p. 7). This kind of research is important for several reasons. It helps demystify the common belief that real research is mostly, if not always, formal, experimental, highly statistical, and conducted by highly trained researchers. This belief is problematic because many teachers see this view of research as intimidating and even scary. One teacher, Brenda Dyck (2004), stated:

> Research always sounded very clinical to me. It was a practice that, along with statistical analysis and mice, belonged in a laboratory, not in my classroom. That was the way I looked at it. I don't look at it like that anymore.
>
> (p. 1)

This teacher shifted her view of research and she is certainly not alone. Increasing numbers of teachers no longer view research as scary or intimidating (Shagoury & Power, 2012). Rather, they see research in more friendly and practical terms, such as "Research is formalized curiosity. It is poking and prying with a purpose" (Hurston, 1996, p. 143). Teacher research invites teachers to see themselves as researchers and inquirers, classrooms as research sites, students as participants, and their own questions as central to teacher growth and development. Kettering (in Lysaker, 2013) describes this shift in thinking as a movement from the yesterday mind to the tomorrow mind.

> Research is a high-hat word that scares a lot of people. It needn't. It's rather simple. Essentially, research is nothing but a state of mind . . . a friendly, welcoming attitude toward change . . . going out to look for change instead of waiting for it to come. Research is an effort to do things better and not to be caught asleep at the switch. It is the problem-solving mind as contrasted with the let-well-enough-alone mind. It is the tomorrow mind instead of the yesterday mind.
>
> (p. viii)

Simply stated, teacher research is important because it pushes back against the notion that real research is only conducted by real researchers and that teachers are consumers, not producers, of research. Teachers should not wait until tomorrow for real research to be passed down to them; rather, they should create it for themselves today.

Lastly, teacher research is important because it situates teachers as researchers and decision makers. All too often, major educational decisions are made *for* teachers, not *by* teachers. While teachers are certainly consulted, decisions about what curricular, instructional, and assessment materials get purchased, as well as what professional development services are contracted, are often made by people other than teachers. Teacher research, however, posits that major decisions should be made by those closest to the learners.

Research Project

We teach graduate courses in literacy education. One course is Reading in the Content Areas. The purpose of this course was to help graduate students gain knowledge about and experience with interdisciplinary curriculum, see what the concept of teacher as researcher looks like when put into action, experience instructional strategies that integrate reading and writing across the curriculum, and provide opportunities for students to actively participate in a teacher as researcher project.

With these goals in mind, we invited students in one class, all of whom are practicing teachers, to participate in a teacher as researcher project. A total of 17 students participated in this project. Of those, six students were practicing elementary (K-4) teachers, 10 were practicing middle grades (5–8) teachers, and one was a practicing high school (9–12) teacher. We invited students to experience an instructional strategy, centered on poetry, that integrated reading, writing, and learning across the curriculum. We wanted participating teachers to actively experience the instructional strategy. We also wanted the experience to be meaningful to them as learners and useful to them as teachers. That is, we wanted them to read and write poems that they could share with their students when using this same instructional strategy in their own classrooms. Lastly, we wanted participating teachers to share their reflections on the experience.

Poetry as a Literary Tool and Flexible Genre

Historically, poetry has been a favorite literary tool to teachers of English-language arts for several reasons. Practically, it is a flexible genre. Poetry uses crafted words, vivid images, interesting rhyming patterns, entertaining rhythmic beats, and invites students to experiment with rhyme, rhythm, repetition, and format (Kane, 1998). Intellectually, it supports abstract thought, provides a means for students to represent and communicate "complex ideas in symbolic ways" (Graves, 1992, p. 163) in a limited amount of space. Poetry also invites students to explore "poetic devices like metaphor, simile, imagery, alliteration, and rhyme and in the process promotes vocabulary development" (Kane & Rule, 2004, p. 665).

Poetry has benefits for interdisciplinary curriculum. Teachers see poetry as a way to teach content area material across the curriculum

(Kane & Rule, 2004). In large part, this is due to the proliferation of high-quality and award-winning literature that uses poetry as a tool to teach across the curriculum. For example, in mathematics, *Edgar Allan Poe's Pie* (Lewis, 2015) is an entertaining and informative collection of math puzzlers, each of which is based on a classic poem such as "The Raven" by Edgar Allan Poe and "April Rain Song" by Langston Hughes. This piece of literature is a wonderful example of the imaginative and informative integration of poetry and mathematics. In science, *Winter Bees & Other Poems of the Cold* (Sidman, 2014) is a collection of poems that describe how a variety of animals (snakes, bees, voles, chickadees) amazingly stay alive during the winter cold. In social studies, A *Wreath for Emmett Till* (Nelson, 2009) is a thought-provoking poem about the murder of Emmett Till, a 14-year-old African American youth, for allegedly whistling at a white woman in 1950s Mississippi. This poem is actually written and illustrated as a crown of sonnets, a sequence of 15 interlinked sonnets.

We used these pieces of literature, and others, to develop and implement an instructional strategy that invited students to use poetry to integrate reading, writing, and learning across the curriculum. We recognize that poetry is not typically a genre used by mathematicians, scientists, and social scientists to convey professional information. However, this strategy focuses on interdisciplinary curriculum, not disciplinary literacy, and uses poetry as a literary tool and flexible genre for students to integrate reading and writing across the curriculum.

Instructional Strategy

We organized this instructional strategy into five stages: (1) initiating; (2) reading, recording, and sharing; (3) reviewing content area literature; (4) writing; and (5) reflecting.

Initiating

Initiating experiences are critically important to successful teaching and learning. The purpose of these experiences was to start with, build on, and extend student current interests. Another purpose was to provide experiences that create student interest and excitement when neither currently exists. Reading aloud a "way-in book" (Bintz, 2011) is a good example of an initiating experience. (Bintz, 2011) states:

> way-in books can interest students in topics for which little or no interest currently exists. Way-in books are high-quality, often award-winning texts that provide students a "way-in"—an unexpected entry into a world of topics they might find interesting to explore.

They are tools for exploration, a way to inquire—an opportunity to pose questions, arouse curiosities, and pursue anomalies about topics of unexpected interest that hopefully will capture their imagination.
(pp. 34–35)

We selected *R is for Rhyme* (Young, 2010) as the way-in book for this project. This beautifully illustrated and informative alphabet book consists of 26 different poems. Each poem uses a different alphabetic letter to describe a specific type of poetic format, terms, and techniques (e.g., B is for ballad, H is for Haiku, L is for Limerick, etc.). For the initiating experience, we read aloud selected poems and the history behind each poetic format. We focused on reading aloud poems with poetic formats that are less common than those typically taught in schools (e.g., Kyrielle, Ghazel, Tyburn, and Senryu). The purpose of this initiating experience was to introduce students to a wide range of familiar and unfamiliar poetic formats, create interest, curiosity, and excitement about poetry, and invite them to explore different poetry formats as models to craft their own poems.

Reading, Recording, Sharing

Reading is a tool to learn and comprehension is the social construction of personal meaning (Harste, Short, & Burke, 1988). Recording and sharing comprehension, especially in writing, allows readers to consider their own and others' perspectives, trace their thought processes, reflect on their understandings, and revisit and reconsider their understandings at other times (Short, Harste, & Burke, 1995). More generally, we see reading as an act of collecting data and comprehension as the data readers collect.

We wanted students to read broadly and deeply, so we developed a text set on poetry across the curriculum (see Appendix A). Collectively, this text set consisted of different kinds of poetic formats. Individually, each text provided an example of a specific poetry format (e.g., renga, or a collection of different formats; haiku, free verse, acrostic, etc.). The purpose of this text set was to provide students with a wide range of reading materials that they could use to re-familiarize themselves with formats already known and/or introduce themselves to unfamiliar and unusual formats.

We divided the text set into five sets (approximately five books per set), organized students in small groups, and invited them to spend time reading through the texts at their table. While reading, students recorded notes about each text, particularly poetry formats that appealed to them. After 20 minutes or so, students rotated their set to another table. This procedure continued until all students read through all of the texts. Afterwards, students shared some of their notes with the whole class. One student noted:

I did not know about Tanka as a poetry form. As I was reading, I jotted down that Tanka and Haiku are similar Japanese forms of poetry. They both deal with nature and have a line-by-line structure. I did not do much poetry in middle school and high school, but I did do Haiku. I wish I knew more about these poetry forms that I never heard of.

Reviewing Content Area Literature

After exploring different poetry formats, we wanted students to integrate a content area emphasis into their thinking. Therefore, we invited them to think about specific content areas as well as high-quality and award-winning literature, primarily picture books, published in that content area that they found appealing. We anticipated, based on our experience teaching this course, that students would have little experience with and knowledge of high-quality and award-winning picture books. Typically, most of their teaching experience comes from using literature in commercial reading programs, content area textbooks, class sets of chapter books, and textbook anthologies.

Therefore, we started by viewing official websites of professional organizations that identify high-quality and award-winning literature for different content areas. In science, we viewed "Outstanding Trade Books for the Teaching of Science" from the NSTA. We also viewed websites from the NCTM, the NCSS, the NCTE, and the IRA. Our purpose was to provide students access to a variety of rich resources from which they could select a high-quality and award-winning piece of literature for this project.

Choice and self-selection both are important to meaningful reading, writing, and learning. Much research indicates that student motivation is a key factor in successful reading (Guthrie et al., 2006). Choice enhances motivation. This is an important—but not new—finding. Studebaker (1977) indicated that choice resulted in students actively reading books from cover to cover. Today, choice still rules, across both gender and age. Essentially, choice enhances reading motivation and encourages readers to engage in more reading. In fact, choice increases reader effort and commitment to reading (Wilhelm & Smith, 2013). Like choice, self-selection is also important. According to the Scholastic Kids and Family Reading Report (2014), "a majority of kids (89%) agree that their favorite books are the ones that they have selected themselves" and "a majority of readers (88%) state that they are more likely to finish books that they pick out themselves (16)."

Writing

We wanted students to integrate reading, recording, sharing, and reviewing with writing. Specifically, we invited them to review their recorded notes, consider their preferences for poetic formats, and revisit content areas they find appealing. Afterwards, we provided students with the following prompt:

> Select one piece of high-quality or award-winning literature from a content area. Then, collect some data. During and/or after reading, jot down all the important ideas you see in this piece of literature. Consider each idea as the basis for a potential poem. Then, select a different poetry format for each idea. For example, you may want to write and illustrate a tanka for one idea, a concrete poem for another, a cinquain for yet another, and so forth. Present your collection of poems in the form of a booklet. Decide which poems from your booklet you wish to share with the whole class.

Reflecting

Like initiating, culminating experiences are critically important to teaching and learning. In many ways, these experiences allow learning experiences to come full-circle, not to end learning but to celebrate and learn from it.

We use reflection as a culminating experience. After a learning experience, we use short prompts to invite students to reflect on their learning. One of our favorite prompts was inspired by the book *The World That Loved Books* (Parlato, 2008). It asked students the simple, but powerful, question: "How are you smarter now as a result of this learning experience?"

In this instance, we invited students to share their selected picture book in small groups and with the class. They also read aloud selected poems from their self-created poetry booklet based on the picture book. We also invited them to write reflections on what they learned from the whole experience.

Writing Samples

Here, we share poems that resulted from this instructional strategy. The poems come from two booklets that represent two different content areas: social studies and science. The majority of booklets were based on these two content areas. We asked students why they focused mostly on social studies and science. One student's response is illustrative:

> "I knew I didn't want to select math. I just don't feel comfortable with my knowledge of math, much less by ability to write poems about math concepts. I really like English-language arts but thought I was already doing ELA by reading and writing poetry. So, I selected social studies and science knowing I was integrating ELA with both."

Social Studies

John (all names are pseudonyms) selected the trade book *Here Comes the Garbage Barge!* (Winter, 2010). This beautifully illustrated book creatively mixes a sense of humor with a serious message about environmental awareness. It is a story about a floating barge loaded with tons of garbage. The captain travels from state to state looking to dump the garbage somewhere, but nobody allowed him. The captain even tries to dump the garbage in Mexico and Belize but militaries turn him away. Finally, the barge is unloaded at an incinerator in Brooklyn, New York. The story reminds people to pay more attention to recycling rather than discarding trash.

His booklet included the following poems: free verse, limerick, haiku, tanka, acrostic, ballad, and diamante. Here, we share his limerick (Figure 5.1), ballad (Figure 5.2), and diamante (Figure 5.3).

He wrote:

> In this limerick, I wanted to create a poem about how littering is damaging to a community and how items can travel from city to city. I wanted to create a similarity between a flying piece of paper and the garbage barge. Just like the barge goes from state to state, the piece of paper goes from park to park. I also wanted to create a similarity between recycling and incinerating garbage, like how the paper could possibly start fresh as a new piece of paper and how the garbage was incinerated for energy.

Traveling Paper

There once was a flying piece of paper

Who had dreams of being a popular newspaper

Until he made his way to the tenth city park

And his dreams of being famous became very dark

He could possibly start fresh as a new piece of paper.

Figure 5.1 Limerick

Pollution

As I was walking in the park

I heard two people talking about an ill shark

One said he had swallowed some plastic

I knew something had to be done drastic.

I learned in closer to hear that many animals were dead

This does not look good in the future ahead

The news reports on the television said

Animals in the water were getting sick from the lead.

With people and agencies trying their best

They worked all day and night with no rest

The cause was factories letting out polluted water

They did not know that this was in the waste water.

Though it has been cleaned up for weeks

There are no smiles on the people's cheeks

For now we can only learn

To try and help the animals return.

Figure 5.2 Ballad

Trash

Trash

Waste, Litter

Collecting, Piling, Overflowing

Building up in landfills, Eventually no more space

Reduce, Reuse, Salvage

Innovative, Inventive

Recycle

Figure 5.3 Diamante

In this ballad, I wanted to inform people about how the news broadcasts information for people to see, but many people do not care about this place because it is too far away. I also wanted to spread awareness that many factories let our pollution into the water and air, but there is little that animals can do about this issue. As concerned people in a community, we can send letters and bring attention to an issue that is threatening an environment. Sometimes it is too late to help a community or an environment and it sometimes takes a while for a group of animals to move back and populate that environment.

In this diamante I wanted to describe how trash can be turned into recycling. The words "waste" and "litter" are associated with trash and can be collected and disposed as garbage. The words "collecting," "piling," and "overflowing" explain how garbage over the years has been accumulating all around us and no one wants garbage. Just like in the story, the garbage barge went all around the nation and two different countries and no one wanted garbage from another place. Recycling is a great way to provide more space for landfills for garbage and provide a way for reusing materials again.

Science

Melissa selected the trade book *No Monkeys, No Chocolate* (Stewart, 2013). This book provides fascinating information about chocolate, how it is made, and who helps make it. Many people know that chocolate comes from cocoa beans from cocoa trees. Fewer people know the important ecosystem (plants and animals) that helps keep these trees alive and flourishing. Monkeys play an incredibly important role in helping cocoa trees to survive, multiply, and ultimately, allow us to enjoy chocolate. The book also provides interesting information about cocoa farming.

Her booklet included the following poems: acrostic, ode, haiku, If I were . . ., tanka, clerihew, and preposition. Here, we share her acrostic (Figure 5.4), If I were . . . (Figure 5.5), and tanka (Figure 5.6).

She wrote:

> I decided to name my acrostic poem "Chocolate" since the main idea of the book is the natural process of making chocolate. I tried to

---

Chocolate

Cocoa beans are a must!

How to find them? Look inside a cocoa pod!

Of course you can't have those without first having flowers.

Cocoa flowers bloom with the help of little midges.

Of course before the flowers, they start out as cocoa leaves.

Leaves soak up the sunlight and some get eaten by the ants, but maggots attack the ants to prevent them from eating all of the leaves.

And the leaves must grow from stems, lizards help to eat pesky bugs off the stems.

The stems can't grow without the roots.

Everything depends on the monkeys who take the pods off of the trees and scatter the cocoa beans to help new trees grow in new places.

Figure 5.4 Acrostic

If I Were a Monkey

If I were a monkey

I would climb up in a cocoa tree

I would find a nice big cocoa pod

And what's inside, I'd want to see.

If were a monkey

I would gnaw holes in the cocoa pod

I would taste the juicy center

The lemony-lime taste would be quite odd.

If I were a monkey

I would swing from tree to tree

I would spit out the beans

So new trees could soon be.

If I were a monkey

I would help new trees grow

I would scatter the beans

My job is important, I know.

Figure 5.5 If I were . . .

From the Ground Up

Big, tall cocoa trees

Strong roots, long stems, bright green leaves

Flowers start to grow

Cocoa pods, fill with small beans

Chocolate can now be made.

Figure 5.6 Tanka

describe each part of the cocoa tree that is essential to its life cycle as well as the living organisms that help it to survive.

In this *If I were . . .* poem, I wanted to explain how a monkey pulls the cocoa pods off of a tree, nibbles holes in them, sucks out the lemony-lime juice, and spits out the beans into the rainforest where eventually new trees will grow. And the process starts all over again.

I decided to write a tanka poem for two reasons. One, I really like the structure, five lines long, first line has five syllables, the second has seven syllables, the third has five syllables, and the fourth and fifth both have seven syllables. Two, I wanted to use that structure to solely focus on just the cocoa tree and its parts, using very descriptive words.

Lessons Learned

This article shared results from a project that used poetry as an instructional strategy to integrate reading and writing across the curriculum. We learned several lessons about integrating reading, writing, learning, and teaching from this project.

In terms of reading, students valued the idea of purposeful reading. In this instance, the purpose was to read and record big ideas in text.

Reading for big ideas, not little ideas, is important. Walmsey (2006) states:

> Many students have well-developed basic literacy skills, but they falter when it comes to critical or thoughtful literacy. Students are quite good at identifying the trivial, but not the substantial—the big ideas! In part, this is due to the fact that engaging students in big ideas is not often a common practice in schools. (p. 281)
>
> Big ideas are often found in texts that have multiple layers of meaning (Peterson & Eeds, 2007). Some meanings are stated explicitly in text; others are stated implicitly and appear under the surface of the text (Walmsey, 2006). Students valued texts with multiple layers of meaning because multiple meanings provided them with multiple options and choices from which to choose.
>
> More specifically, students noticed a key characteristic of high-quality and award-winning pieces of literature; namely, this literature has multiple layers of meaning. They started to understand that literature with multiple layers of meaning offered readers an opportunity to comprehend a text from multiple perspectives.

One student stated:

> After reading and thinking about my book, I realized that I could read it from different perspectives and see new possibilities from it. For example, my book focused on the need for recycling, not discarding trash. I started to think though that incinerating trash produces energy and that got me thinking about our need for alternative sources of energy like solar instead of coal. I also started to think about environmental issues other than recycling, like the difference between regeneration and extinction. Environmental regeneration is hopeful but takes time; extinction is hopeless because it is gone no matter how much time.

Multiple perspectives enable students to actively engage with a text and make sense of a text by thinking, wondering, connecting, and reflecting during and after reading. In this instance, students made personal connections to different texts and related these connections to local, national, and even global settings.

In terms of writing, students learned a variety of poetry formats and then selected different formats to represent and communicate the big ideas of a text. Students were thoughtful and reflective about how different poetry formats offered different ways to communicate ideas. In other words, different poetry formats allowed them to represent different meanings. In this sense, they were strategic about selecting and using different formats for different ideas and also intentional about their selection of words and how these words were used in poems. Inquiry, knowledge, and creativity were all integrated.

One student stated:

> After reading my book about chocolate several times, one of the things I started to realize was how people, including me, often take a common thing like chocolate for granted and think of it so simplistically, like a favorite treat. I learned that chocolate, how it is made, and who makes it is really important and complex. I kept the idea of complexity in mind as I started to select which poetic formats I wanted to use. I wanted the formats to capture the complexity.

In terms of learning, students actively experienced the power and potential of interdisciplinary curriculum. Specifically, they experienced the value of integrating reading, writing, and learning across the curriculum. Like them, we learned how interdisciplinary curriculum and instructional strategies like the one described in this research project are not just important, they are necessary.

Different poetic formats, however, do not just involve various literary forms or poetic structures. They offer students opportunities to be creative, weigh choices, consider options, take different perspectives, and see different viewpoints. Integrated teaching and learning like this is not clean and streamlined; it is messy and recursive. Providing students choice and self-selection invites them to be inquirers and direct their own learning by integrating thinking, wondering, connecting, solving problems, taking action, deal with decisions, valuing difference, and reflecting on their own learning.

In terms of teaching, this kind of instructional strategy, and many others like it, benefits all students, especially young adolescents. A fundamental tenet of middle-level education is to teach the whole child, not individual parts of a child (National Middle School Association, 2010). Likewise, a fundamental tenet of interdisciplinary curriculum is to teach a whole curriculum in an integrated way, not teach individual content areas (Olness, 2007). For students, interdisciplinary curriculum helps them understand the world in an integrated, non-fragmented, way. It also allows them to see and experience learning in complex ways.

For teachers, interdisciplinary curriculum offers potential and opportunities not possible with disciplinary curriculum. It broadens and extends the possibilities for curriculum and instruction rather than narrowing them. Moreover, it opens up new possibilities for how teachers think about and use time. For example, instead of viewing literacy as a separate content area with a separate block of time, teachers can see literacy as an academic discipline in the service of other disciplines. Thus, literacy is a tool to help students learn science, social studies, mathematics, career and technical education, etc. One student, who teaches middle grades science, stated:

> We are departmentalized at my school. Until now, I've only had limited experience integrating literacy across the curriculum. I've always seen literacy and science as separate content areas, but now I can see how literacy is a tool that can help students better learn any content area, including science.

Lastly, we learned that shifting from a disciplinary to an interdisciplinary view of curriculum invites teachers across the curriculum to open their doors to colleagues, rather than close them so they can do their own thing. Opening doors is meant to be literal and metaphorical. Opening doors allows teachers across the curriculum to talk, hear new voices, start new conversations, and collaborate on developing and implementing integrated curriculum. Ultimately, however, opening doors allows teachers an opportunity to explore an alternative way of thinking about what kind of professional lives we want to live. One student, who teaches middle grades social studies, stated:

> I teach social studies because I really like it. I am comfortable with helping my students read social studies, but am not comfortable with helping them write about it. In part, I think that's because I don't know many writing strategies that would really engage my students. This experience has really opened my eyes about writing across the curriculum. I never would have thought about using poetry in my social studies class. I want to share this experience with English teachers at my school and see if we can start collaborating more across our content areas.

Next Steps

One of our goals was to demonstrate to our students that developing interdisciplinary curriculum and integrated instruction are not "superhuman feats, but natural extensions of good teaching practice and conversations among colleagues" (Galles, 2005, p. 12). Another goal was to provide students with an integrated experience that they would value enough to share with their own students. As one student said:

> I loved this experience. It is an experience I would definitely bring to my own classroom because, for one thing, I believe now more than ever in the value of my students having choice and self-selection in their academic work. I think that giving them choice and self-selection allows them to feel ownership and really helps them to feel more

engaged in learning. I think that this experience, and others like it, will have a positive impact on student learning.

We also hope this experience leads to next steps for us and other teacher educators. There are many other possibilities for this kind of classroom-based research project with preservice and in-service teachers. One possibility is to use this instructional strategy with multicultural literature to not only integrate English-language arts but also multicultural education across content areas. Multicultural literature has been described as providing windows and mirrors through which students can not only see themselves and their world, but also see other people and the worlds in which they live (Bishop, 1997). Students can write poetry based on self-selected pieces of multicultural literature as a way to provide mirrors for themselves and windows for others.

Another possibility is to use this instructional strategy for change and social justice. Adolescents are interested in contemporary social issues across the curriculum, especially controversial ones. Students can read high-quality and award-winning literature about a variety of social issues. They can self-select an issue that is important to them, immerse themselves in focused readings and research about the issue, and then write and share advocacy poems that seek to enlighten, clarify, or transform. This adaptation makes curriculum personally relevant and academically rigorous, as well as allows students to feel empowered, experience active engagement, and see literacy as a tool for social change.

Many other possibilities exist. For now, we hope this article starts new conversations about how teachers can create curriculum that is challenging, exploratory, integrative, and relevant.

References

Akins, A., & Akerson, V. L. (2002). Connecting science, social studies, and language arts: An interdisciplinary approach. *Educational Action Research*, *10*(3), 479–497. https://doi.org/10.1080/09650790200200196

Bintz, W. P. (2011). "Way-In" books encourage exploration in middle grades classrooms. *Middle School Journal*, *42*(3), 34–45.

Bintz, W. P., & Moore, S. D. (2005). What's up with sinking? *Science and Children*, *43*(1), 20–22.

Bishop, R. S. (1997). Selecting literature for a multicultural curriculum. In V. J. Harris (Ed.), *Using multiethnic literature in the K-8 classroom* (pp. 1–19). Norwood, MA: Christopher Gordon.

Cochran-Smith, M., & Lytle, S. (1992). *Inside/Outside: Teacher research and knowledge*. New York: Teachers College Press.

Dewey, J. (1910). *How we think*. Lexington, MA: DC Heath and Company.

Dyck, B. (2004, August). Me? A teacher-researcher? *Education World*. Retrieved from www.educationworld.com/a_curr/voice/voice135.shtml

Fang, Z., & Ashley, C. (2004). Preservice teachers' interpretations of a field-based reading block. *Journal of Teacher Education, 55*(1), 39–54. https://doi.org/10.1177/0022487103259814

Galles, J. (2005). Interdisciplinary does not mean intimidating. *The Science Teacher, 72*(8), 12.

Graves, D. (1992). *Explore poetry*. Portsmouth, NH: Heinemann Educational Publishers.

Guthrie, J. T., Wigfield, A., Humenick, N. M., Perencevich, K. C., Taboada, A., & Barbosa, P. (2006). Influences of stimulating tasks on reading motivation and comprehension. *The Journal of Educational Research, 99*(4), 1–15. https://doi.org/10.3200/JOER.99.4.232-246

Harste, J., Short, K., & Burke, C. (1988). *Creating classrooms for authors*. Portsmouth, NH: Heinemann.

Heimer, L., & Winokur, J. (2015). Preparing teachers of young children: How an interdisciplinary curriculum approach is understood, supported, and enacted among students and faculty. *Journal of Early Childhood Teacher Education, 36*(4), 289–308. https://doi.org/10.1080/10901027.2015.1100144

Hurston, Z. N. (1996). *Dust tracks on a road*. Minneapolis, MN: Tandem Library.

International Technology and Engineering Educators Association. (2000). Retrieved from www.iteea.org

Kane, S. (1998). Teaching skills within meaningful contexts. *The Reading Teacher, 51*(5), 434–436.

Kane, S., & Rule, A. C. (2004). Poetry connections can enhance content area learning. *Journal of Adolescent & Adult Literacy, 47*(8), 658–669.

Lachapelle, C. P., Sargianis, K., & Cunningham, C. M. (2013). Engineer it, learn it: Science and engineering practices in action. *Science and Children, 51*(3), 70–76. https://doi.org/10.2505/4/sc13_051_03_70

Lewis, J. P. (2015). *Edgar Allan Poe's pie: Math puzzlers in classic poems*. Boston, MA: Harcourt Children's Books.

Lysaker, J. T. (2013). *Teacher inquiry in literacy workshops: Forging relationships through Reggio-inspired practice*. Urbana, IL: National Council of Teachers of English.

Morgan, E., & Ansberry, K. (2015). Every part has a purpose. *Science and Children, 52*(7), 16–22. https://doi.org/10.2505/4/sc15_052_07_16

National Middle School Association. (2010). *This we believe: Keys to educating young adolescents*. Westerville, OH: Association for Middle-level Education.

Nelson, M. (2009). *A wreath for Emmett Till*. Orlando, FL: HMH Books for Young Readers.

Olness, R. (2007). *Using literature to enhance content area instruction: A guide for K-5 teachers*. Newark, DE: International Reading Association.

Parlato, S. (2008). *The world that loved books*. Vancouver, Canada: Simply Read Books.

Peterson, R., & Eeds, M. (2007). *Grand conversations*. New York: Scholastic.

Richards, J. C., & Shea, K. T. (2006). Moving from separate subject to interdisciplinary teaching: The complexity of change in a preservice teacher K-1 early field experience. *The Qualitative Report, 11*(1), 1–19.

Romance, N. R., & Vitale, M. R. (1992). A curriculum strategy that expands time for in-depth elementary science instruction by using science-based reading strategies: Effects of a year-long study in grade four. *Journal of Research in Science Teaching, 29*(6), 545–554. https://doi.org/10.1002/(ISSN)1098-2736

Royce, C. A., & Wiley, D. A. (2005). The common ground: A rationale for integrating science and reading. *Science and Children, 28*(6), 40–42.

Scholastic. (2014). *Kids & family reading ReportTM: Fifth edition.* Commissioned by Scholastic and conducted by YouGov. New York: Scholastic, Inc.

Shagoury, R., & Power, B. M. (2012). *Living the questions: A guide for teacher-researchers.* Portland, ME: Stenhouse Publishers.

Short, K., Harste, J., & Burke, C. (1995). *Creating classrooms for authors and inquirers.* Portsmouth, NH: Heinemann.

Sidman, J. (2014). *Winter bees and other poems of the cold.* Orlando, FL: HMH Books for Young Readers.

Stenhouse, L. (1983). *Authority, education and emancipation: A collection of papers by Lawrence Stenhouse.* Portsmouth, NH: Heinemann Educational Publishers.

Stewart, M. (2013). *No monkeys, no chocolate.* Watertown, MA: Charlesbridge.

Studebaker, J. (1977). *The love to read: Report on a study of paperback book clubs in classrooms of five cities.* New York: Scholastic.

Walmsey, S. (2006). Getting the big idea: A neglected goal for reading comprehension. *The Reading Teacher, 60*(3), 281–285. https://doi.org/10.1598/RT.60.3.9

Weinberg, A. E., & Sample McMeeking, L. B. (2017). Toward meaningful interdisciplinary education: High school teachers' views of mathematics and science integration. *School Science and Mathematics, 117*(5), 204–213. https://doi.org/10.1111/ssm.2017.117.issue-5

Wilhelm, J., & Smith, M. (2013). *Reading unbound: Why kids need to read what they want—And why we should let them.* New York: Scholastic.

Winter, J. (2010). *Here comes the garbage barge.* New York: Schwartz & Wade.

Young, J. (2010). *R is for rhyme: A poetry alphabet.* Ann Arbor, MI: Sleeping Bear.

Appendix A
Text Set of Poetry Across the Curriculum

Crew, G. (1998). *Troy Thompson's excellent poetry book*. La Jolla, CA: Kane/Miller.

Dotlich, R. K., & Yoshikawa, S. (2006). *What is science?* New York, NY: Henry Holt and Company.

Fleischman, P. (1985). *I am phoenix: Poems for two voices*. New York, NY: HarperCollins.

Fleischman, P. (1988). *Joyful noise: Poems for two voices*. New York, NY: HarperCollins.

Fleischman, P. (2000). *Big talk: Poems for four voices*. Cambridge, MA: Candlewick.

Hopkins, L. B. (2006). *Got geography!* New York: Greenwillow Books.

Lendroth, S. (2005). *Why explore?* Berkeley, CA: Tricycle Press.

Lewis, J. P. (1998). *Doodle dandies*. New York, NY: Scholastic Inc.

Lewis, J. P. (1998). *The house of boo*. New York, NY: Atheneum Books for Young Readers.

Lewis, J. P. (2002). *A world of wonders*. New York: Dial Books for Young Readers.

Lewis, J. P. (2003). *Swan song*. Mankato, MN: Creative Edition.

Lewis, J. P. (2005). *Please bury me in the library*. Orlando, FL: Gulliver Books.

Lewis, J. P. (2009). *The house*. Mankato, MN: Creative Editions.

Lewis, J. P. (2015). *Edgar Allan Poe's pie: Math puzzlers in classic poems*. Boston, MA: Harcourt Children's Books.

Lewis, J. P., & Janeczko, P. B. (2008). *Birds on a wire*. Honesdale, PA: Wordsong.

Mannis, C.D., & Hartung, S. K. (2002). *One Leaf Rides the Wind*. New York, NY: Viking Children's Books.

Michelson, R. (2000). *Ten times better*. New York, NY: Marshall Cavendish.

Pappas, T. (1991). *Math talk: Mathematical ideas in poems for two voices*. San Carlos, CA: Wide World Publishing/Tetra.

Sandburg, C. (1970). *Arithmetic*. San Diego, CA: Harcourt Brace Jovanovich.

Schnur, S. (2001). *Summer: An alphabet acrostic*. New York, NY: Clarion Books.

Scieszka, J. (2004). *Science verse*. New York, NY: Viking Books for Young Readers.

Sidman, J. (2000). *Just us two: Poems about animal dads*. Brookfield, CT: The Millbrook Press.

Sidman, J. (2005). *Song of the water boatman and other pond poems*. Boston, MA: Houghton Mifflin Company.

Sidman, J. (2016). *Before morning*. Orlando, FL: HMH Books for Young Readers.

Vergo, F. (2012). *Sciencepalooza: A collection of science poetry for primary and intermediate students*. Bloomington, IN: AuthorHouse.

Winston, L., & Hoberman, M. A. (2009). *The tree that time built: A celebration of nature, science, and imagination*. Naperville, IL: Sourcebooks Jabberwocky.

Wold, A. (2003). *The blood-hungry spleen and other poems about our parts*. Cambridge, MA: Candlewick Press.

Yolen, J. (2000). *Color me a rhyme: Nature poems for young people*. Honesdale, PA: Wordsong.

Yolen, J. (2009). *A mirror to nature: Poems about reflection*. Honesdale, PA: Wordsong.

Young, E. (2005). *Beyond the great mountains: A visual poem about China*. San Francisco, CA: Chronicle Books.

6 Rethinking Content Teaching at the Middle-Level

An Interdisciplinary Approach

Kelly M. Moser, Jessica Ivy, and Peggy F. Hopper

This We Believe Characteristics

- Educators value young adolescents and are prepared to teach them.
- Curriculum is challenging, exploratory, integrative, and relevant.
- A shared vision developed by all stakeholders guides every decision.

Middle-level learners represent a diverse group of individuals between the ages of 10 and 14 who experience significant changes in terms of cognitive, social, emotional, and physical development. Integrative planning and teaching may assist educators in addressing these unique needs. The position statement, *This We Believe*, by the Association for Middle-Level Education (formerly National Middle School Association) (National Middle School Association, 2010) highlights this method as a crucial aspect of the middle school concept. Specifically, curricula for the middle level should be "challenging, relevant, integrative, and exploratory" (National Middle School Association, 2010, p. 17). Integrative teaching (e.g., interdisciplinary, multidisciplinary, cross-disciplinary, etc.) has been linked to numerous characteristics that may benefit middle-level learners including increased student engagement, motivation, and achievement (Applebee, Adler, & Flihan, 2007) as well as the synthesis of knowledge that comes from exploring topics and ideas through multiple lenses (Lee, 2007). For the purposes of this collaborative project, we define *interdisciplinary* loosely based on the definition from The National Academy of Sciences (2004, p. 2) as "two or more disciplines" that together work "to advance fundamental understanding . . . beyond the scope of a single discipline or area. . . ." Although the middle school concept certainly emphasizes the role of discipline integration, the focus on integrating content is also evident in the core content standards (English-Language Arts, Foreign Language, Mathematics, Science, and Social Studies). For example, the following terms are highlighted as part of these content standards: *cross-disciplinary connections* (Foreign Language), *interdisciplinary applications* (Social Studies), *sequence of learning in all content areas* (Science), *representation and connections* (Math), and *synthesis*

(English) (See American Council on the Teaching of Foreign Languages, 2015; National Council for the Social Studies, 2013; National Council of Teachers of English/International Reading Association, 1996; National Council of Teachers of Mathematics, 2000; NGSS Lead States, 2013). Further, the Common Core State Standards (National Governors Association Center for Best Practices & Council of Chief State School Officers, 2010) encourage teachers to work collaboratively. As one source described teachers' actions embracing the Common Core State Standards, "Rather than tackling these new objectives in subject-area silos, some teachers are choosing to address them by integrating real-world themes and social issues into projects, and by reaching across hallways to do this work with colleagues" (Heitin, 2013, p. 4). Prior to the change in standards and the advent of the Common Core, integrated curricula at the middle level was still relatively rare (Beane, 1991; Schwartze & Hatch, 2015). Recent research also suggests that many middle-level structures such as integrated teaching are "limited, absent, or not fully implemented" (Ellerbock & Kiefer, 2014, p. 233).

As a result of engaging in multiple discussions about these content standards and in response to the realization that we were working as insular "silos," the secondary education faculty decided to work together to alter our teaching practices. Our goal was ultimately to change our own perspectives about interdisciplinary teaching that would then transform our students who will be future teachers.

Like many states, the institution in which we work does not have a fully implemented middle-level teacher preparation program (Howell, Faulkner, Cook, Miller, & Thompson, 2016). Thus, the important responsibility of preparing future middle school teachers falls upon faculty in both elementary education, who work with candidates seeking licensure in grades K-6, and secondary education, who prepare those individuals pursuing 7–12 certification. Further, we recognize the need to provide candidates with high-quality middle-level-relevant coursework and field experiences, especially since among the 16 teacher preparation programs in the state of Mississippi, only one requires at least one course/experience-related specifically to the middle grades (Howell et al., 2016). This reality serves as the justification for our project that required our preservice teachers to focus on middle-level challenges such as the breadth of learners' cognitive abilities in a classroom, social and emotional development that often contribute to peer pressure, outbursts, and feelings of anxiety, and searching for one's identity.

Method

Although the purpose of our work was to improve our teaching practice, to do so, we relied on an action research process. Our goal was twofold—to improve our preservice teachers' experiences in their programs of study and to provide them with more quality models of middle-level teaching which we had already identified as absent and/or limited in our own program of study. Preservice teachers completed a variety of tasks, all of which we used during data collection as relevant artifacts, including written reflections, lesson and unit plans, poster presentations, and discussions with interdisciplinary members. While tasks varied throughout the semester, we did our best to catalog these accurately, and we met and reflected both individually and collectively as faculty. Further, each component of the project and of our data collection connected to the questions that guided our inquiry:

- What do preservice teachers know about interdisciplinary teaching?
- How prepared are our preservice teachers to engage with middle-level learners?
- What gaps exist in our programs of study that might better equip preservice teachers to work with middle-level learners?

What follows is a description of a collaborative project initiated in the secondary content specific methods courses taught by the authors. As is characteristic of integrative curricula, teachers and students collaborated, engaged in reflective practice, and learned together. In the upcoming sections, we analyze our experiences with this project from our own perspectives and from those of our students. Our interpretation of what students learned is based on their written reflections throughout the project as well as observing and entering in discussions with them. In addition, we provide suggestions for other teacher educators who wish to engage in similar interdisciplinary projects.

The Interdisciplinary Unit Project

The interdisciplinary unit project (IUP) was a collaborative effort by all secondary faculty involved in teaching methods courses across a variety of disciplines. The first of two methods courses in each discipline at our institution integrates topics related to and experiences with middle-level learners and serves as an introduction to standards in each discipline. Given the importance of cross-disciplinary connections previously discussed, faculty engaged in multiple discussions to plan for opportunities for learners to design tasks around interdisciplinary themes using suggestions from Powell (2015) that emphasize concepts rather than content as central thematic features. Faculty also chose to divide all students enrolled in a methods class into interdisciplinary groups consisting of four individuals each when possible, which represents the optimal grouping for secondary content experts (Wallace,

2007). Additionally, we hoped to create groups representing each of the disciplines of our students.

Once per month, in addition to regularly scheduled methods class meetings, faculty co-taught lessons to the combined cohort of students and provided immediate and delayed feedback as they worked through a variety of unit-based tasks (e.g., standards exploration, choosing an interdisciplinary theme, connecting their theme to multiple disciplinary standards, designing essential questions and assessments, and creating individual lesson plans). Faculty also designed each task to deconstruct the three stages of Understanding by Design (Wiggins & McTighe, 2005) into smaller teachable parts and allowed our students to enact specific instructional skills as a result (see Figure 6.1).

Prior to each combined session, faculty met to discuss the project, plan the upcoming sessions, address student or faculty concerns, and select tasks and relevant readings with a focus on equitably sharing the workload and sequencing instruction appropriately. Although faculty received no course releases for collaborating on and implementing this project, faculty proceeded with a common understanding and commitment that participating in the IUP would benefit the teaching and learning of future middle grade teachers. Faculty were involved at every stage of the project by providing feedback during discipline-specific methods classes and through multiple iterations of the IUP tasks with the entire cohort. In the following sections of this paper, we provide concrete examples of experiences and suggestions for others who may consider a similar endeavor.

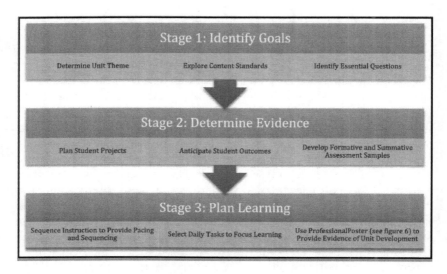

Figure 6.1 Alignment to Understanding by Design

Standards Exploration

Because we identified gaps in our knowledge base related to disciplines other than our own, we anticipated that our students would also be unfamiliar with the expectations of other disciplines. Hence, the first task required students to engage in an exploration of standards (see Figure 6.2). Students served as both experts (by assisting their group members with details of their own standards) and as novices when relying on their classmates for guidance in uncharted territory. Students also considered how they might collaborate with teachers of other disciplines by hypothesizing about topics that crossed typical content area boundaries.

Student Experiences: Increasing Awareness of Disciplinary Standards

In general, this exploratory task benefitted all students. Although previous coursework required our students to use these standards to create multiple artifacts such as lesson plans, units, and assessments, we found that students were concerned that they were not very knowledgeable about their own content standards, much less the standards of other areas. As one student, Michael, shared, "I learned a great deal about creating a lesson plan based on the use of standards. Before the IUP project, I had never used standards for anything or even done a lesson plan on my own. . . ." (Reflection Response One). Similarly, Carla reflected,

> I also learned how to incorporate Common Core Standards in my lesson planning. I had never used this skill before, and honestly I was a little weary (sic) of it. This project helped me become more comfortable with navigating the standards.
>
> (Reflection Response Two)

Although it was beneficial overall, our students questioned the relevance of this exploratory task and understanding standards outside of their specific disciplines. Eventually, however, they grew to understand the value as evidenced from the following student examples. Tara wrote,

1. Briefly examine the **2014 MS College and Career Readiness Standards for Mathematics**. List the five mathematical domains for grade 7 and the five mathematical domains for grade 8.
2. Compare the two lists from item 1. Describe what you notice.
3. List the eight **Standards for Mathematical Practice**. How are these different from the content standards?

Figure 6.2 Standards Exploration: A Scavenger Hunt, Mathematics Questions

It was also valuable to me because this allowed me the opportunity to find new ways that different content areas can connect. I always understood how English and Social Studies could connect, but this allowed me to understand how math and science could, as well"

(Reflection Response One)

Calvin offered:

In addition, I value the experience I got from not just working with other people but working with other disciplines that I am not very knowledgeable in. I learned how teachers in other disciplines operate in forming lesson plans and making a unit that reaches into other disciplines to give students a well-rounded educational experience.

(Reflection Response One)

Students also hypothesized about the difficulty or ease related to working with one another once in the classroom as practicing teachers. For example, students in mathematics were more likely to share stories and ideas related to working with teachers in science, and individuals in the social studies more frequently offered examples integrating English-language arts. The literature reflects these particular pairings (Applebee et al., 2007). Thus, one of our challenges was to encourage and assist our students to think beyond these typical combinations. For example, Bailey wrote, "The IUP gave me insight into other concentrations besides English. I was able to make connection(s) between my content area, English and science" (Reflection Response One).

Faculty Experiences: Identifying Gaps in Student Knowledge

By observing our students working with the standards, we found that students often lacked significant understandings or expressed misconceptions about their own content area standards—an issue we had not anticipated because of their consistent exposure to disciplinary standards throughout earlier education coursework. For example, students often required much assistance to respond to prompts even with a content area "expert" present in their group. "Experts" often were unsure of where to find answers, were hesitant to provide their classmates with the answer, or only had superficial understandings of their standards. For example, students would misinterpret a standard requiring application or evidence of conceptual understanding to mean recall of a formula (i.e., eighth grade students should understand and apply the Pythagorean theorem; however, students interpreted this as recalling the standard formula for the Pythagorean theorem and applying it in a limited, textbook-style problem). As faculty, we are accustomed to addressing these misconceptions;

however, we typically do so within our own insular methods courses rather than in the interdisciplinary setting.

Interestingly, while faculty designed the project to integrate collaborative teaching and planning, we found that we ultimately completed this first task of creating the interdisciplinary scavenger hunt individually. Rather than looking at all the standards as a group, for instance, we returned to our isolated subjects and drafted questions/prompts based on our understandings of our own standards. As a result, ingrained practices that were very difficult to alter initially thwarted the goal of our project.

Advantages of Collaboration Across Disciplines

Because the ultimate goal of our project was to collaborate with one another and to encourage our students to do so as well, we suggest beginning in this way. The standards exploration task sets the stage for all future collaborative tasks. It would have been more successful if individuals from all disciplines designed it together rather than separately. As teacher educators, had we explored the standards together, we might have also come to an understanding early on about the expectations across disciplines at a variety of levels and how to design short-term and long-term learning experiences using this information. Further, because we design our discipline-specific courses around program standards tightly aligned to these student standards, a thorough understanding of all disciplinary standards might assist us in developing uniform expectations of all our students, regardless of discipline.

Additionally, providing concrete examples to students following the exploration of standards might assist them in seeing the value of this type of work while also serving as a tool for identifying standards. For example, students might read a learning scenario that integrates mathematics and social studies and identify the standards addressed throughout that experience.

Choosing an Interdisciplinary Theme

After students became more familiar with the disciplinary standards, we recognized that they needed to begin their unit by identifying an interdisciplinary theme. Faculty first required students to read selected articles related to these tasks. Additionally, we distributed a unit example related to the Holocaust in which learners would consider the governmental system in Germany and causes and effects of mass genocide (social studies), anaerobic and aerobic respiration and nutrition/malnutrition (science), ratios and probability (mathematics), and the implications of the text *Night* by Elie and Marion Weisel (English-language arts) (Weisel & Weisel, 2006). The purpose of the unit plan was for learners to explore themes that cross typical disciplinary boundaries such as racism, power, human rights, privilege, and xenophobia through multiple lenses.

In class, students engaged in discussions related to the readings and examples, and they then considered themes using their own standards as a guide (Figure 6.3). Initially, we did not provide a definition for interdisciplinary themes to students which would distinguish a theme from a content topic, aside from directing students to identify a theme that connected to the content areas represented in their group. Perhaps our Holocaust example misguided students into thinking that an event was the only or best way to create an interdisciplinary unit. To prevent confusion, faculty could have created a list of potential themes in advance and students could have selected their group's theme from this predetermined list; however, we believe this would have limited their agency and creativity.

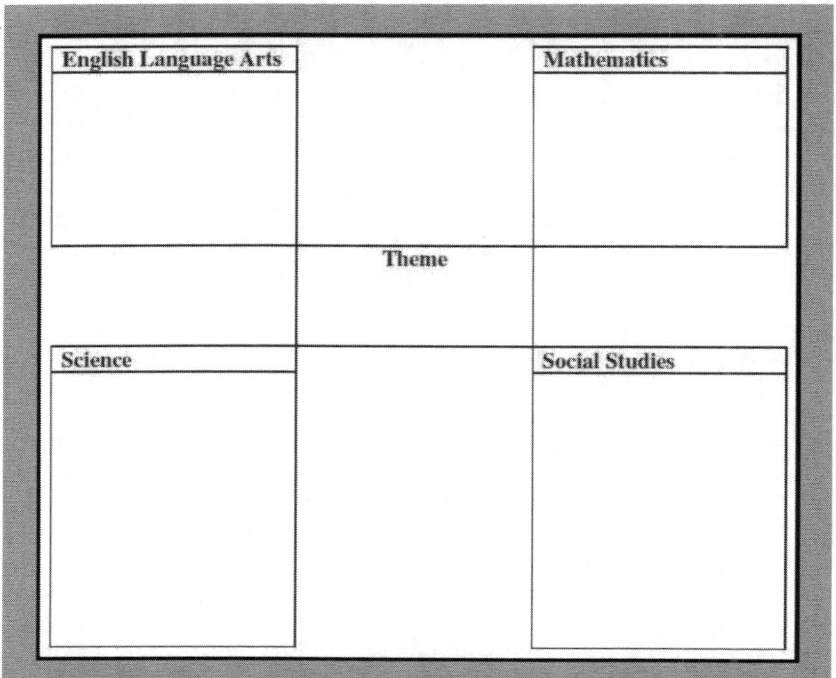

Figure 6.3 Connecting Disciplines to a Central Theme

To offer more guidance, we later communicated to students that an effective theme would draw on the interests of students, connect to multiple content areas with balance across those areas, and foster collaboration.

Student Experiences: Challenging Preconceived Notions About Themes

The identification of themes was a particularly difficult task for our students. For example, Sheila shared, "My greatest challenge was finding a lesson/topic that would match the overall theme to the best of my ability" (Reflection Response Three). Similarly, Allison asserted, "Coming up with a theme was the most difficult part because there are so many things to consider" (Reflection Response Three).

Although we set up a graphic that allowed students to show how the theme connected to the represented disciplines, we found the initial submissions were lacking in interdisciplinary connections. Rather, the proposed themes lent themselves strongly to the social studies with many centered on a notable event in history (see Figure 6.4). Following initial feedback, we realized that students needed much more guidance. Hence, we provided questions to engage each group in more detailed discussions so they could direct their focus toward conceptual issues

	Original Theme	Revised Theme	Essential Question(s) for Revised Theme
Group 1	Vietnam War	The Wall	How do walls solve and create problems?
Group 2	Revolutionary War	Mississippi Poverty	How did poverty shape Mississippi, and how is it still shaping it?
Group 3	Civil War	Social Media	What does it mean to communicate responsibly via social media? How does communication impact personal relationships?

Figure 6.4 Evolution of Themes

rather than begin with historical events (e.g., what are students interested in currently? What are larger societal issues—local, regional, national? What are controversial issues worth discussing?). These questions guided our students to more broadly consider their middle-level learners' interests, social conflicts, big ideas, and culturally relevant pedagogy. This assistance led to an evolution of conceptual themes that was more in line with our expectations (Figure 6.4). The changes of theme were primarily based on a consideration of student interests and broadening their original theme. For example, the group that originally selected the Vietnam War revised their theme to "The Wall", a broader approach to considering both real walls and those obstacles which are more abstract.

Although theme identification was certainly challenging for our students, it appeared that the majority understood its importance in unit design. According to Jennifer, "I realized how tough it is to find a common theme between every subject matter, [but] it gave me a new set of skills to think deeper in a lesson plan than just educating students in my own subject" (Reflection Response One). This student's response is indicative of this being their first opportunity to plan with backwards design in a thoughtful and reflective manner. Students completed tasks at each phase of the project and reflected to gain these transferable skills. Paul also commented,

> It was valuable to see how difficult it is to tie subjects together with a theme. I found it mind opening to think through the process of making the connections. I hope to be able to use this process in my classroom.
>
> (Reflection Response One)

Faculty Experiences: Reconciling Conflicting Expectations

At times, faculty seemed to hold different ideas of what an appropriate theme for interdisciplinary unit design might be. This occurred when a theme provided some clear integration of some disciplines but not others, and the faculty who felt their represented discipline would determine the unit inappropriate. Since faculty were considering the themes from the lens of their represented discipline, this was less of a surprise for faculty than for students. This finding led to frustration for students as they sought approval from all secondary education faculty prior to beginning their units. Marcos explained,

> Whenever we chose our overarching theme, . . . there was confusion. During that meeting, we were to go meet with our content experts and get them to sign off on it. . . . We got approved from two experts.

Then, we were told to change our theme by the third. . . . There should have been one person approving each theme.

(Reflection Response Three)

The different expectations (not solely those related to theme identification) by faculty seemed to be a common concern of both students and faculty. Faculty, however, identified this concern early on in the project and considered it to be an area for future improvement and growth as a collaborative unit. For example, one faculty member shared, "I valued the project discussions and the opportunity to listen to my colleagues discuss their approach to coursework, teaching, grading, and interdisciplinary work" (Reflection Response). Another offered, "It allowed me to learn about what my colleagues do in their courses and to reflect on my own practice. I was able to consider excellent ideas/strategies that my colleagues use when teaching" (Reflection Response). In future iterations of this project, during initial theme selection, students will learn that they may receive conflicting feedback from faculty. Also, this process has allowed faculty to establish some common understandings and to better agree on feedback and expectations.

Advantages of Collaboration

Given students' initial difficulty with theme selection and their focus on historical events, future iterations of this project would include providing multiple types of examples. Another exercise that might support theme selection could be for students to identify their disciplinary standards in various examples before our discussion on interdisciplinary themes. Thus, students would have multiple ways of interacting with interdisciplinary examples, standards, and themes prior to producing their own work.

Unexpected Outcomes

Repeatedly throughout the project, several themes emerged that were not tied specifically to one task. These frequent and often unexpected outcomes were related to collaboration and trust. In a sense, we *did* expect a level of required collaboration from the students; however, the collaboration as a faculty group was unique, valuable, and surprising. As one faculty member stated, "I found it worthwhile to collaborate across disciplines. In secondary education, we are often very isolated because our disciplines require us to meet different standards. I think the project forced us to work more like a cohesive unit" (Reflection Response). As faculty who often collaborate more on issues of policy than the content we teach, the project provided a basis for gaining insight into other disciplines and an appreciation for the challenges and successes we each face in our work with pre-service teachers. Likewise, the pre-service teachers grew to appreciate their peers in other content areas, viewing them as resources and respecting their contributions as classroom teachers and classroom managers. As Jamie wrote,

> I find it valuable that now I know more secondary education majors from a discipline other than my own. That may sound strange, but I think it's important that we get out of the bubble of our discipline sometimes. When we do that, we get to appreciate the work others do and just see more of what our future students will be learning.
> (Reflection Response One)

Trust grew immensely among the faculty and student groups. Faculty agreed the project felt risky from the sense of students, but we also agreed to trust each other and listen to the varying perspectives. As pre-service teachers' frustrations grew at times, faculty met to consider these sentiments and to share ideas for encouraging perseverance. We each had our own unique approaches and procedures, but the project allowed us to step back, trust one another, and learn more about one another and ourselves. The pre-service teachers also grew to trust each other, and later reflected that the process very much mimicked expectations in their local middle-level internship experiences, where there was an expectation that teachers would breach the content barriers they often self-imposed and rely on and trust one another.

As Calvin said, "If I was ever stumped on a certain aspect of one of the tasks, I knew I could trust the advice of my peers. Learning to trust the knowledge and advice of others will go a long way in shaping me to be a well-rounded teacher" (Reflection Response Two).

The structure of the project appeared to also promote this sense of trust among students and faculty. Upon reflecting the project, it became clear that this finding was likely due to our collective desire for success. Students realized that for their units (and thus their future instruction) to be effective and reflect good pedagogy grounded in adolescent development, they needed to work together and trust that each participant contributed to the success of the whole group. We reflected this in our faculty collaborations as well. We hoped that students would mimic our collaborative work once in their classrooms as practicing teachers.

Many times, the difficulties associated with collaborative work became transparent to students. While we certainly had not intended on displaying these challenges to our students, it appeared to benefit them in many ways. First, it increased trust between students and between students and faculty, and second, it led to a sense of belonging to a *middle-level cohort* with common goals rather than to isolated secondary disciplines. On many occasions, faculty admitted when they were unsure of their colleagues' expectations or when confusions arose because of disparate responses to student questions. The truthfulness of the faculty group regarding making and learning from mistakes likely led our students to trust us as fallible individuals who ultimately wanted them to be excellent educators, often requiring them to admit and learn from errors. Further, faculty discourse in front of students displayed a negotiation of ideas and expectations that we student reflected in their discussions.

Conclusion

This project originated as a way to better prepare preservice secondary teachers to address the unique needs of middle-level learners. Through this experience, preservice secondary teachers were able to explore these needs while collaborating across disciplines to create units, which integrated content in meaningful ways. Students' perceived difficulty collaborating beyond their isolated discipline reflects real-world classroom scenarios— where there is an expectation that teachers will do so with ease.

Candidates gained knowledge about the meaning of interdisciplinary instruction and planning and gained skills in collaborating with teachers of other disciplines. Certainly, the lessons created in this project reflected the novice nature of the students (see Figures 6.5 and Figure 6.6 for samples of final projects); however, it also provided a foundation that reflected the value in teaching with an approach that is more comprehensive and less insular. From the perspective of faculty, we quickly identified gaps in our own knowledge base. We were previously unaware of the expectations of our colleagues in their various methodology courses as well as had limited understandings of disciplinary standards other than our own.

Overall the project highlighted our commonalities and our uniqueness and provided a springboard for future efforts as well as the value of having a unified voice for our future teachers. Although we were unable to do so given time constraints, further iterations of this project will require our preservice teachers to seek feedback from middle grades teachers, revise their thematic units, and implement these units in middle grades classrooms during their field experiences. Despite continuing to operate somewhat individually upon the conclusion of this experience, this project has highlighted the specific need to work on interdisciplinary efforts as we prepare middle-level teachers. Further, this introduces a need for a separate course with integrated field experiences, addressing the complexities of planning interdisciplinary lessons for middle-level learners. Currently, this project has led to further curricular exploration and discussion.

STAGE 1: IDENTIFY DESIRED RESULTS

THEME: Exploration Beyond the Classroom

ENDURING UNDERSTANDINGS:
Students need to understand the problem presented and can defend their opinions on the impacts of exploration. Afterwards they should devise a plan on how to tackle or solve the problem, and then carry out and defend their plan. Finally, reflect on their process and revise when necessary.

ESSENTIAL QUESTIONS: What are the impacts of explorations?

Discipline 1	Discipline 2	Discipline 3
Enduring Understandings Understanding figurative language, critical thinking, and essay writing strategies in regards to our works focused on exploration.	**Enduring Understandings** Understand and make sense of exploration problems and persevere in methods of solving the problem. Understand how to problem solve and think critically, while reasoning abstractly and quantitatively. Understand and make use of mathematical structure in exploration problems.	**Enduring Understandings** Students should be able to critically understand the causes and impacts of a historical event specifically in regards to American exploration.
Standards / Skills *Homesick*- Erin Hanson (R1) *The Road Not Taken*- Robert Frost (R4/ L5/W3) *If*- Rudyard Kipling (R2)	**Standards / Skills** Explain and apply the Pythagorean Theorem using the idea of the different paths traveled. 8.G.6, 8.G.7, 8.G.8 Analyze and solve linear equations and pairs of simultaneous linear equations. We will pull in different paths traveled and we can mathematically represent them. 8.EE.7, 8.EE.8	**Standards / Skills** Western expansion and immigration in the United States •2.B, 2.C, 5.B
Essential Questions Where are you going? How are you going to get there? Who do you want to be when you get there?	**Essential Questions** What is the quickest route? What path did you travel?	**Essential Questions** Why, how, and to what ends have Americans explored?

UbD Stage 2 Scoring Guide:

Item	Points Possible	Points Earned
A performance task is described in the table. Copies of the task sheets (instructions provided to middle school students) are attached to the submission.	1	
One test or quiz item is included.	1	
At one academic prompt is included.	1	
A description of one informal check is included.	1	
All assessment items appropriately connect to the theme.	1	
All assessment items address disciplinary standards.	1	
Each standard is represented at least once in the Task 2 table.	2	
Task is submitted on time.	1	
Template is used and directions are followed. Task is submitted on time. Writing is accurate (spelling, grammar, syntax, punctuation, etc.)	1	
TOTAL	**10**	

Figure 6.5 Sample Unit Template

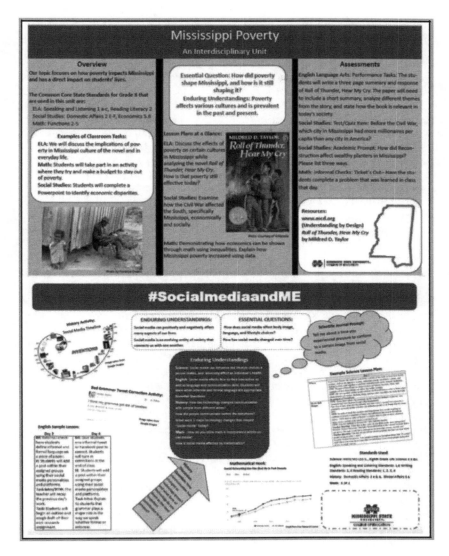

Figure 6.6 Project Samples: Poster Design

References

American Council on the Teaching of Foreign Languages. (2015). *World-readiness standards for learning languages* (4th ed.). Alexandria, VA: National Standards in Foreign Language Education Project.

Applebee, A. N., Adler, M., & Flihan, S. (2007). Interdisciplinary curricula in middle and high school classrooms: Case studies of approaches to curriculum and instruction. *American Educational Research Journal, 44*(4), 1002–1039. https://doi.org/10.3102/0002831207308219

Beane, J. (1991). The middle school: The natural home of integrated curriculum. *Educational Leadership, 19*(2), 9–13.

Ellerbock, C., & Kiefer, S. (2014). Fostering an adolescent-centered community responsive to student needs: Lessons learned and suggestions for middle level educators. *The Clearing House, 87*(6), 229–235. https://doi.org/10.1080/0009 8655.2014.933157

Heitin, L. (2013). In common core, teachers see interdisciplinary opportunities. *Education Week: Teacher.* Retrieved from www.edweek.org/tm/articles/2013/03/13/ccio_interdisciplinary_units.html

Howell, P., Faulkner, S., Cook, C., Miller, N., & Thompson, N. (2016). Specialized preparation for middle level teachers: A national review of teacher preparation programs. *Research in Middle Level Education, 39*(1), 1–12. https://doi.org/10.1080/19404476.2016.1226100

Lee, M. (2007). Spark up the American revolution with math, science, and more. *The Social Studies, 98*(4), 159–164. https://doi.org/10.3200/TSSS.98.4.159-164

National Academy of Sciences. (2004). *Facilitating interdisciplinary research: National academies of science, national academy of engineering, and institute of medicine of the national academies.* Washington, DC: The National Academies Press.

National Council for the Social Studies. (2013). *The college, career and civic life (C3) framework for social studies state standards: Guidance for enhancing the rigor of K-12 civics, economics, geography, and history.* Silver Springs, MD: NCSS.

National Council of Teachers of English/International Reading Association. (1996). *The standards for the English language arts.* Urbana, IL: NCTE.

National Council of Teachers of Mathematics. (2000). *Principles and standards for school mathematics.* Reston, VA: Author.

National Governors Association Center for Best Practices & Council of Chief State School Officers. (2010). *Common core state standards for English language arts and literacy in history/social studies, science, and technical subjects.* Washington, DC: Authors.

National Middle School Association. (2010). *This we believe: Keys to educating young adolescents.* Westerville, OH: Author.

NGSS Lead States. (2013). *Next generation science standards: For states, by states.* Washington, DC: The National Academies Press.

Powell, S. D. (2015). *Introduction to middle level education* (3rd ed.). New York: Pearson.

Schwartze, M., & Hatch, D. (2015). Common core standards & interdisciplinary instruction: Do common core standards help or hinder interdisciplinary instruction? *AMLE Magazine.* Retrieved from www.amle.org/BrowsebyTopic/WhatsNew/WNDet/TabId/270/ArtMID/888/ArticleID/514/Common-Core-Standards-Interdisciplinary-Instruction.aspx

Wallace, J. (2007). Effects of interdisciplinary teaching team configuration upon the social bonding of middle school students. *Research in Middle Level Education Online, 30*(5), 1–18.

Weisel, E., & Weisel, M. (2006). *Night.* New York: Hill and Wang.

Wiggins, G., & McTighe, J. (2005). *Understanding by design* (2nd ed.). Alexandria, VA: ASCD.

7 A Community and Place-Based Approach to Middle Childhood Science Teacher Education

Danielle Dani

This We Believe Characteristics

- Educators value young adolescents and are prepared to teach them.
- Curriculum is challenging, exploratory, integrative, and relevant.
- A shared vision developed by all stakeholders guides every decision.
- The school includes community and business partners.

The Association for Middle-Level Education (formerly National Middle School Association) (National Middle School Association [NMSA], 2010) calls for middle grades education that is developmentally appropriate, challenging, empowering, and equitable. The realization of this vision of education necessitates a prepared and knowledgeable teaching force whose members create and enact equitable and relevant curriculum that nurtures the development of all children and adolescents. The AMLE Middle-Level Teacher Preparation Standards call for middle-level teachers who understand young adolescent development, understand the implications of diversity on young adolescents, and "implement curriculum and instruction that is responsive to young adolescents' local, national, and international histories, language/dialects, and individual identities" (Association for Middle-Level Education [AMLE], 2012, p. 1).

Middle-level teacher education programs across the nation attend to the essential attributes of middle grades education through coursework and field experiences by focusing on social foundations of education, child and adolescent development, and culturally responsive teaching. In school-based clinical experiences, teacher candidates learn about students, the school context, and in rare occasions, the ways in which the larger local community can be used to enrich student learning. Consequently, the majority of coursework and field experiences seem to occur in separate locales: university (Colleges of Education and Colleges of Arts and Science) and PK-12 schools. This separation results in a disjointed teacher education curriculum that lacks connections and coherence between university-based courses and school-based field experiences (Darling-Hammond, 2006; Zeichner, 2010).

To prepare teachers to implement curriculum and instruction that is responsive to young adolescent local identity, middle grades teacher education must occur across these institutional boundaries and develop teacher candidates' knowledge of the places in which the university and schools exist. Using the construct of place to design learning experiences for middle grades teacher candidates empowers them to leverage local culture and community to create relevant curriculum and learning experiences for all middle grades students.

This article describes several evidence-based strategies to promote a place-based approach to middle-level teacher education that capitalizes on the local context and community to actualize the middle school philosophy. The strategies can also be used by middle grades teachers to promote place-based teaching and learning in middle school classrooms.

Place-Based Education

According to Semken and Freeman (2008), place-based education is an instructional method that involves experiential learning in and about local or regionally characteristic natural and social settings; transdisciplinary and cross-cultural synthesis of place-related knowledge and pedagogy; and service learning or other forms of community outreach. As a philosophical orientation, place-based teaching and learning emphasizes the study of socio-spatial context, and particularly local community, as a focus of formal education (Hutchinson, 2009). It represents a cross-cultural and multi-disciplinary approach to teaching that immerses learners in local heritage, culture, ecology, landscapes, opportunities, and experiences as a foundation of language arts, mathematics, social studies, science, and other subjects (Hutchinson, 2009). The situated experiential approach to place-based teaching turns communities into classrooms by encouraging teacher educators, teachers, and students to use the community, public lands, and other special places as nested resources to promote formal school learning (Buxton & Provenzo, 2012).

In practice, place-based education engages learners in exploring the local context in one of five different ways: culture studies, nature studies, internship and entrepreneurial opportunities, real-world problem-solving and issue investigations, and participation in community decision-making processes (Smith, 2002). It differs from other inquiry-based and experiential approaches through its emphasis on the study of place. Place-based education programs have a positive effect on student learning and achievement, student behavior, and community engagement (Lieberman & Hoody, 1998; Powers, 2004). The approach engenders a commitment to educating whole citizens who think critically about local and global issues. The approach further develops self-directed students and teachers who are creative problem solvers as well as active participants in their communities (Smith & Sobel, 2010). Place-based education has the potential to erase the barrier between the school and the community and promote the social construction of places, place identity, place attachment, and a sense of place (Gruenewald, 2003a). Gruenewald (2003b) proposed the notion of a critical pedagogy of place whereby learners take a transformative role as they (a) examine marginalizing practices prevalent in a place, (b) identify the links between such practices and oppression, and (c) "change ways of thinking that exploit other people and places" (p. 9). To realize the transformational potential of place-based education for middle-level learners, teachers must be aware of placed-based pedagogies and know the places where they teach.

Knowledge of place is critical to promoting teacher candidates' understanding of the sociocultural context and when considering student learning in authentic settings. By connecting to the community where their students live, teacher candidates can develop "powerful, transferable, and useful" experiences for learning (Basu & Barton, 2007, p. 468). They then develop into community teachers who connect their practice to broader movements for social justice (Kretchmar & Zeichner, 2016). A place-based approach to teacher education provides teacher candidates the opportunities to develop place consciousness (White & Reid, 2008).

The following sections describe how place-based education can be used to engage middle-level science teacher candidates in studying local place and community, get to know their students, and learn strategies for developing and enacting middle-level curriculum. Strategies include photovoice journaling and using citizen science or problem-based learning to co-teach with community partners. Specific examples are shared to illustrate how each strategy was used to support middle-level science teacher education in the context of a science methods course at a large, rural, Midwestern university.

Photovoice Journaling

Photovoice was originally developed by Wang and Burris (1994) as a research design and methodology that involves participants in taking photographs about personal and community issues that are important to them, and then using the photos as the basis for critical discussion and social change. Inspired by the work of Goldston and Nichols (2009), who used photonarratives to investigate black middle school teachers' ideas about culturally relevant pedagogy, a journaling project was created to engage teacher candidates in photovoice research to interrogate their beliefs about students and place through a process of becoming more knowledgeable about them. Using this method, participants act as co-researchers who investigate a question that is of value to them (e.g., lake quality, what it means to be healthy). The strategy has been success-fully used with middle school learners in both formal (Cook & Buck, 2010) and informal educational contexts (Farley, Brooks, & Pope, 2017; Strack, Magill, & McDonagh, 2004; Wilson et al., 2007; Zenkov & Harmon, 2009).

The Middle Childhood Education Science Methods photovoice journal project was focused on two questions:

1. What community referents pose barriers to teaching and learning science?
2. What community references build bridges for teaching and learning science?

Before beginning the journaling project, 17 teacher candidates learned about the photovoice methodology and discussed the guiding research questions. Because the photovoice journaling project was designed using the methodology of photovoice, teacher candidates engaged in photo-voice research as they completed the following activities. To create their journals, teacher candidates took pictures of places and events in the school community and logged the reasons for taking pictures, the day, time, and place of the picture. Teacher candidates spoke to community members, including students and school personnel, to learn about the places and events they photographed. Photographs depicted landmarks that spoke about the community's history (see Figure 7.1), scenic natural resources (see Figure 7.2), homes, restaurants, and markets, and other places and landmarks with cultural (see Figure 7.3), ecological, or social significance. Teacher candidates concluded their photovoice journals with a narrative that described what they learned about the local community. For example, one teacher candidate wrote:

> [The] county was a very large source of coal production beginning in the late nineteenth century, up until the early 1990s. I did not know this, and the students were excited to tell me! I encouraged the students to tell me more about coal mining. The students stated that they know coal is burned to produce energy, and this coal is obtained from deep in the ground. One student talked about the movie *October Sky* and how this made him "proud" to live where he lives.

In the university classroom, teacher candidates worked in teams (based on field placement locales) to share and discuss photovoice journals and the patterns or themes that, as a group, they saw emerge from their

Figure 7.1 Mining and Labor Mural Within the Community

Figure 7.2 Natural Resources Within a Local State Park

narratives about each place. In response to the research questions, each team then presented their stories about each place to the class. With support from the course instructor, teacher candidates unpacked stories at each locale and compared stories across locales to identify how their

Figure 7.3 Apple Festival Water Tower

personal experiences, stereotypes, and biases affected their perceptions of the bridges and barriers to the teaching and learning of science. During these theme-building sessions, teacher candidates not only identified new learning about the places in and around the school-community, but also new learning about themselves, their assumptions, and biases.

The photovoice journal project concluded with a written reflection in which teacher candidates described what they learned, how their ideas changed, and how they would use the new knowledge to create equitable and challenging curriculum for middle-level learners at their schools. This required teacher candidates to develop interdisciplinary lessons that utilized community places and included standards-aligned learning outcomes for three different disciplines (science and two more). For science, the lessons targeted Next Generation Science Standards (NGSS) earth, life, and physical science performance expectations for students in grades 5–8 (NGSS Lead States, 2013). As a learning activity, the photovoice journaling project promotes a critical examination of place, leads to the development of a strong sense of place, allows teacher candidates to design equitable learning experiences, and equips teacher candidates with the tools and skills to use similar approaches to learn about the students, communities, and places in which they will teach. A key to the success of the photovoice journaling project was the requirement to connect with and learn from community members. The following sections describe how such informal connections can transform into formal partnerships to promote placed-based teacher education.

Partners in Place

In schools across the nation, material resources continue to diminish because of state and federal budget cuts as well as an eroding tax base (Strange, Johnson, Showalter, & Klein, 2012). In sparsely populated rural areas, this problem is exacerbated and affects instructional expenditures (Biddle & Azano, 2016; Strange et al., 2012). In the midst of these increasing financial constraints, it is crucial that teachers utilize educational resources in their community to create meaningful learning opportunities for their students. Partnerships with community organizations can be developed to capitalize on the expertise of private and public community agencies and groups, the richness of the local area, develop teacher candidates' sense of place, and support teacher candidates' learning about a variety of STEM teaching approaches. Using such university-community partnerships to facilitate university course teaching provides teacher candidates with a model of the ways in which community partners can enrich the science curriculum by helping them promote learning about the natural resources in their place. In the following sections, partnerships focused on citizen science and problem-based learning are described.

Citizen Science

Citizen science is a type of scientific research that is conducted by the public (i.e., children, adolescents, young adults, and adults who are not scientists) who then share their results with researchers who are interested in the topical field of study. Various well-established citizen science projects exist worldwide, collecting observations about a variety of organisms and natural phenomena including monarch butterflies, stardust, frogs and toads, and birds (e.g., Great Backyard Bird Count; Cornell, n.d.). Citizen science promotes more meaningful learning because it allows learners to make "connections between the data, their community, and environmental health" (Jenkins, 2011, p. 507).

Several educators have used citizen science projects with middle school students and teacher candidates. Projects include examining invasive turtle species and their effects on native turtle species (Dohrenwend, 2012) and pollution by plastic pellets (Summers, 2012). Hiller and Kitsantas (2014) found that middle school students who engaged in a citizen science project about horseshoe crabs reported higher self-efficacy, interest, and academic performance when compared with students who learned about horseshoe crabs in the science classroom. Scott (2016) engaged her elementary teacher candidates in collecting data about turtles and uploading the data to a citizen science database. In addition to learning about citizen science projects and reptiles, Scott reported that future teachers developed "a sense of social responsibility . . . and a desire to teach students about the importance of local environment" (p. 37).

To introduce the MCE teacher candidates to citizen science, the Science Methods course instructor, a member of the local birding society, and a non-profit organization focusing on local development developed a partnership. The purpose of the partnership was to provide teacher candidates with more meaningful connections to science and the rural community in and around the university through citizen science. During the science methods course, partners provided a brief introduction to the work of citizen science, shared example projects, and situated each project within the NGSS (NGSS Lead States, 2013). Then, partners engaged teacher candidates in collecting data about local birds, bird nests, and other flora and fauna in the community using mobile citizen science applications (e.g., iNaturalist) and walks through local neighborhoods. Community partners explained local bird conservation initiatives such as Nest Box, identified birds that were seen or heard, described the status of each type of bird population and factors that affected the health of the population in the region (e.g., habitat destruction, pollution, disease, and climate change), and invited teacher candidates to observe other plants and animals that were native or non-native to the region.

As teacher candidates engaged in citizen science, they communicated with the larger local community by posting pictures of interesting and unknown living things they saw on the walk and receiving responses from iNaturalist members who helped identify their organisms. In addition to engaging first hand in citizen science experiences and developing the ability to integrate such experiences in their future classrooms, this university-community partnership demonstrated to teacher candidates how local experts and community members can support their learning (and their future students' learning) about local environments, flora, and fauna. The methods course instructor was not an expert in birds and was new to the practice of citizen science. Through this partnership, the instructor was able to model how to be a learner alongside your students, ask key questions to connect to the science curriculum, and use the field and community-based experiences as a springboard for further learning about teaching. This partnership also illustrated a model of coteaching that transcends the school or university walls. The next section describes how partnerships can support place-based education by engaging in issue investigation, problem-solving, and decision-making.

Problem-Based Learning

Problem-based learning environments provide students with real-world opportunities to investigate phenomena and answer questions about them (Sutton & Knuth, 2017). Problem-based learning invites learners to consider various perspectives as they ask, "who benefits" from these decisions and actions, as well as who is "harmed" by the same. Problem-based learning additionally promotes student achievement, engagement, and motivation of all students (Sutton & Knuth, 2017).

Sustainability, a community and university-wide emphasis, was selected as the locally relevant problem to investigate. Teacher candidates toured university facilities such as the Ecohouse and the Compost Facility and participated in a class presentation and discussion about sustainability in their lives and their profession as science teachers. Back in the methods classroom, teacher candidates learned about socio-scientific issues, which are complex social dilemmas that impact economic, civic, and cultural affairs; lack clear-cut solutions; and have conceptual or technological ties to science (Sadler, 2004). To further investigate composting, the methods course instructor collaborated with a community member and business owner who farmed and sourced red wiggler worms to engage the MCE teacher candidates in evaluating the sustainability of the practice of composting from a social, economical, and ecological perspective (Dani, 2011) and to practice composting. Teacher candidates used information gathered from university resources (e.g., the benefits of using the nutrient-rich soil amendment that results from composting on university grounds and selling it to the public) and community resources (e.g., city-wide composting services) to determine advantages and challenges as well as the impacts of composting related practices and results on various community stakeholders. Then, teacher candidates set up their own compost bins, investigated different approaches to composting (with and without red wiggler worms), donated the resultant compost to the university gardens, and developed interdisciplinary and standards-aligned lessons to engage middle school students in learning about composting and sustainability.

Relatedly, students engaged in problem-based learning focusing on designing garden plots and using them as spaces to learn about core science and interdisciplinary content. Groups of future teachers were given a plot of land to prepare, dig, plant, and care for throughout the semester. Not only did teacher candidates engage in investigations of local produce and ecosystems, they also developed standards-aligned, STEM-focused, literacy-infused, and collaboration-rich curricula around the processes and products of gardening and the diverse ecosystem of gardens. Teacher candidates discussed the advantages and challenges to engaging students in similar types of learning using school gardens.

Many researchers have used local gardens as spaces to promote diversity pedagogies like culturally responsive teaching (Gay, 2010). School gardens foster students' sense of place and provide them access to the diverse linguistic, ethnic, and cultural backgrounds that can inform learning (Williams & Anderson, 2015). Using school gardens as sites for problem-based learning creates opportunities for families, caregivers, and community members to be partners in the education of the community's children. In short, problem-based learning is an effective strategy for promoting place-based education for middle-level students and teacher candidates alike.

Conclusion

This article presents several strategies for integrating place-based education into the educator preparation process (e.g., photovoice, partnerships for citizen science, and partnerships for problem-based learning). Place-based education can demonstrate to future science teachers one of the key characteristics of successful middle schools—how to connect with families, community, and business partners to promote personal and community health and wellness (National Middle School Association, 2010). Place-based education aligns with the goals of justice-oriented teacher education by requiring that the places of teacher education shift from traditional institutions to "multiscaped geographies" that can occur within and beyond educational contexts (Jones & Hughes, 2016, p. 179; Jones, 2012). A place-based approach strengthens science teacher education by engaging candidates in service learning projects that take them out of formal educational contexts and into the community, position them as learners who benefit from the expertise and funds of knowledge present in the places they inhabit, and create opportunities for them to give back to the community to further educational growth and development (Ball & Geleta, 2012; Moll, Amanti, Neff, & Gonzalez, 1992).

Through their preparation programs, teacher candidates must learn about the history and context of a local place and community as well as how to leverage this knowledge to design and enact empowering curriculum that builds on students' lived experiences. The resulting deep knowledge of a community, its history, and its context can disrupt science teacher candidates' existing stereotypes and biases and interrogate deficit perspectives of people and places. Additionally, a place-based approach to science teacher education supports the development of culturally relevant teaching practices (Gay, 2010).

Engagement in community-based and locally relevant problems also promotes social problem-solving, which is interdisciplinary by nature and capitalizes on the tenets of a middle school curriculum. The interdisciplinarity inherent to place-based education stems from the traditional and non-traditional types of knowledge that Zeichner (2010) deemed necessary for justice-oriented teaching: academic, practitioner, and community-based knowledge. The context-specific (as opposed to decontextualized) nature of place-based education enables teacher candidates to answer the critically important "so what?" question that speaks to the relevance of the curriculum they teach. The context-specific social problem-solving afforded by place-based education can foster teachers who are transformers and change agents (Cochran-Smith, 1991; Kretchmar & Zeichner, 2016).

While the examples provided in this manuscript are science specific, both the strategies and examples can be used to support middle childhood teacher preparation for other disciplines, including language arts, mathematics, and social studies. Place-based education strategies and examples like the ones described herein are relevant to middle grades teachers as well. Middle grades teachers can use place-based teaching strategies to develop and enact interdisciplinary curriculum that is locally relevant. Place-based education can allow teachers to implement the middle school philosophy even when the middle school organizational structure is absent. Place-based education is interdisciplinary, creates space and opportunity for teaming, and capitalizes on community partnerships.

References

Association for Middle Level Education. (2012). *Association for middle level education middle level teacher preparation standards with rubrics and supporting explanations*. Westerville, OH: Author.

Ball, D., & Geleta, N. (2012). A delicate balance: Service-learning in teacher education. *Journal of the Scholarship of Teaching and Learning, 5*(1), 1–17.

Basu, S. J., & Barton, A. C. (2007). Developing a sustained interest in science among urban minority youth. *Journal of Research in Science Teaching, 44*(3), 466–489. https://doi.org/10.1002/(ISSN)1098-2736

Biddle, C., & Azano, A. P. (2016). Constructing and reconstructing the "rural school problem": A century of rural education research. *Review of Research in Education, 40*(1), 298–325. https://doi.org/10.3102/0091732X16667700

Buxton, C. A., & Provenzo, E. F. (2012). *Place-based science teaching and learning: Activities for K-8 classrooms*. Washington, DC: Sage Publications.

Cochran-Smith, M. (1991). Learning to teach against the grain. *Harvard Educational Review, 61*(3), 279–311. https://doi.org/10.17763/haer.61.3.q671413614502746

Cook, K., & Buck, G. (2010). Photovoice: A community-based socio-scientific learning tool. *Science Scope, 33*(7), 35–39.

Cornell University. (n.d.). *The great backyard bird count*. Retrieved from www.birdsource.org/gbbc

Dani, D. (2011). Sustainability as a framework for analyzing socioscientific issues. *International Journal of Environmental Education, 2*, 113–127.

Darling-Hammond, L. (2006). *Powerful teacher education: Lessons from exemplary programs*. San Francisco, CA: Jossey-Bass.

Dohrenwend, P. (2012). Citizen science international pellet watch. *Science Scope*, *36*(3), 50–53.

Farley, L., Brooks, K., & Pope, K. (2017). Engaging students in praxis: Using photovoice research. *Multicultural Education*, *24*(2), 49–52.

Gay, G. (2010). *Culturally responsive teaching: Theory, research, and practice* (2nd ed.). New York: Teachers College Press.

Goldston, M. J., & Nichols, S. (2009). Visualizing culturally relevant science pedagogy through photonarratives of Black middle school teachers. *Journal of Science Teacher Education*, *20*, 179–198. https://doi.org/10.1007/s10972-009-9125-z

Gruenewald, D. A. (2003a). Foundations of place: A multidisciplinary framework for place-conscious education. *American Educational Research Journal*, *40*(3), 619–654. https://doi.org/10.3102/00028312040003619

Gruenewald, D. A. (2003b). The best of both worlds: A critical pedagogy of place. *Educational Researcher*, *32*(4), 3–12. https://doi.org/10.3102/0013189X032004003

Hiller, S. E., & Kitsantas, A. (2014). The effect of a horseshoe crab citizen science program on middle school student science performance and STEM career motivation. *School Science and Mathematics*, *114*(6), 302–311. https://doi.org/10.1111/ssm.2014.114.issue-6

Hutchinson, D. (2009). Place-based education. In E. F. Provenzo, J. P. Renaud, & A. B. Provenzo (Eds.), *The encyclopedia of the social and cultural foundations of education* (Vol. 2). Thousand Oaks, CA: Sage Publications.

Jenkins, L. L. (2011). Using citizen science beyond teaching science content: Making science relevant to students' lives. *Cultural Studies of Science Education*, *6*(2), 501–508. https://doi.org/10.1007/s11422-010-9304-4

Jones, S. (2012). Trauma narratives and nomos in teacher education. *Teaching Education*, *23*(2), 131–152. https://doi.org/10.1080/10476210.2011.625087

Jones, S., & Hughes, H. E. (2016). Changing the place of teacher education: Feminism, fear, and pedagogical paradoxes. *Harvard Educational Review*, *86*(2), 161–182. https://doi.org/10.17763/0017-8055.86.2.161

Kretchmar, K., & Zeichner, K. (2016). Teacher prep 3.0: A vision for teacher education to impact social transformation. *Journal of Education for Teaching*, *42*(4), 417–433. https://doi.org/10.1080/02607476.2016.1215550

Lieberman, J., & Hoody, L. (1998). *Closing the achievement gap: Using the environment as an integrating context for learning*. San Diego, CA: State Education and Environmental Roundtable.

Moll, L., Amanti, C., Neff, D., & Gonzalez, N. (1992). Funds of knowledge for teaching: Using a qualitative approach to connect homes and classrooms. *Theory Into Practice*, *31*(2), 32–141. https://doi.org/10.1080/00405849209543534

National Middle School Association. (2010). *This we believe: Keys to educating young adolescents*. Westerville, OH: Author.

NGSS Lead States. (2013). *Next generation science standards: For states, by states*. Washington, DC: The National Academies Press.

Powers, A. (2004). An evaluation of four place-based education programs. *The Journal of Environmental Education*, *35*(4), 17–32. https://doi.org/10.3200/JOEE.35.4.17-32

Sadler, T. D. (2004). Informal reasoning regarding socioscientific issues: A critical review of research. *Journal of Research in Science Teaching*, *41*(5), 513–536. https://doi.org/10.1002/(ISSN)1098-2736

Scott, C. M. (2016). Using citizen science to engage preservice elementary educators in scientific fieldwork. *Journal of College Science Teaching*, 46(2), 37. https://doi.org/10.2505/4/jcst16_046_02_37

Semken, S., & Freeman, C. B. (2008). Sense of place in the practice and assessment of place-based science teaching. *Science Education*, 92(6), 1042–1057. https://doi.org/10.1002/sce.v92:6

Smith, G. A. (2002). Place-based education: Learning to be where we are. *Phi Delta Kappan*, 83(8), 584–594. https://doi.org/10.1177/003172170208300806

Smith, G. A., & Sobel, D. (2010). *Place and community-based education in schools*. New York: Routledge.

Strack, R. W., Magill, C., & McDonagh, K. (2004). Engaging youth through photovoice. *Health Promotion Practice*, 5(1), 49–58. https://doi.org/10.1177/1524839903258015

Strange, M., Johnson, J., Showalter, D., & Klein, R. (2012). *Why rural matters 2011–12: The condition of rural education in the 50 states*. Washington, DC: Rural School and Community Trust.

Summers, S. (2012). Turtle conservation and citizen science: A winning combination for your classroom. *Science Scope*, 36(3), 33–38.

Sutton, P. S., & Knuth, R. (2017). A schoolwide investment in problem-based learning. *Phi Delta Kappan*, 99(2), 65–70. https://doi.org/10.1177/003172 1717734193

Wang, C., & Burris, M. A. (1994). Empowerment through photo novella: Portraits of participation. *Health Education & Behavior*, 21(2), 171–186.

White, S., & Reid, J. (2008). Placing teachers? Sustaining rural schooling through place-consciousness in teacher education. *Journal of Research in Rural Education*, 23(7), 1–11.

Williams, D., & Anderson, J. (2015). Tongue-tied no more: Diversity pedagogy and sense of place in the learning gardens. *Canadian Journal of Environmental Education*, 20, 25–45.

Wilson, N., Dasho, S., Martin, A. C., Wallerstein, N., Wang, C. C., & Minkler, M. (2007). Engaging young adolescents in social action through photovoice. *Journal of Early Adolescence*, 27(2), 241–243. https://doi.org/10.1177/02724 31606294834

Zeichner, K. (2010). Rethinking connections between campus courses and field experiences in college- and university-based teacher education. *Journal of Teacher Education*, 61(1–2), 89–99. https://doi.org/10.1177/0022487109347671

Zenkov, K., & Harmon, J. (2009). Picturing a writing process: Photovoice and teaching writing to urban youth. *Journal of Adolescent & Adult Literacy*, 52(7), 575–584. https://doi.org/10.1598/JAAL.52.7.3

Index

Page numbers in italics indicate figures and in bold indicate tables on the corresponding pages.